OUR LAND
OURSELVES

Dear Keith   7/21/00

It is an honor greater
than words to have you in
such an important role in
my wedding! We are very
fortunate to have such amazing
family members.

With much love —
Theres —
Chi

OUR LAND, OURSELVES

Readings on People and Place

Second Edition

Editors

✦

Peter Forbes
Ann Armbrecht Forbes
Helen Whybrow

The Trust for Public Land

SAN FRANCISCO, CALIFORNIA

→>-<+-

"By perceiving ourselves as part of the river, we take
responsibility for the river as a whole."

—VACLAV HAVEL

→>-<+-

This anthology is dedicated to all those whose love of the land leads them each day to do the hard work of land conservation, and the good work of expanding the American commons.

Contents

I : OUR CHALLENGE

Chapter 1: Does Land Conservation Matter? . 7

Chapter 2: A Rolling Stone Gathers No Moss · 27

III : TOWARD A NEW LAND ETHIC

Chapter 6: Good Work · 115

Chapter 7: Home · 133

Chapter 8: Storytelling · 161

Acknowledgments

"Success is never final, failure is never fatal.
Courage is the only thing."

—WINSTON CHURCHILL

+>-<+

When this anthology was first conceived and presented to The Trust for Public Land in the winter of 1998, it was something of a daunting proposition: let's fully examine our values and purpose as a conservation organization. What you hold in your hands is a book whose original purpose was to begin our own questioning process as a movement, and what supported that, as well as its life now as a book for all to read, is the courage and participation of a great many people. Within TPL, the effort would never have gone beyond an idle thought were it not for the leadership and support of Will Rogers, Ralph Benson, and Lisa Cashdan. This anthology bears the mark of the good work of Susan Ives, Alan Front, Kathy Blaha, Chris Mann, Valerie Talmage, Molly Paul, Julie Iffland, Anne Truslow, Shaun Hamilton, Al Raymond, Ted Harrison, Sandy Tassel, Kathrynn Drahn, Scott Parker, Nelson Mathews, Ann Cole, Dave Sutton, Suzanne Moss, Bowen Blair, Chris Beck, Peter Scholes, Chris Rogers, Geoff Roach, Rose Harvey, Erik Kulleseid, Will Abberger, Dale Allen, Rand Wentworth, Doug Raff, Doug Ferguson, Lester Abberger, David Getches, Polly Cross Reeve, Liz Uhlin, and Tony Wood.

Many individuals outside of TPL lent their enthusiasm, intellectual vigor, and critical perspective to give the anthology a bigger view, a larger mountain to scale. These important catalysts include Ian Baldwin, Bill Coperthwaite, William Cronon, Charles Geisler, Michel Gelobter, John Kauffman, Stephen Kellert, Chuck Matthei, Dana Meadows, David Orr, Marc Roberts, and John Saltmarsh. Thanks also to Jenna Dixon, Dean Bornstein, and Helen Whybrow for their tremendous help in the production phase of this project.

Leadership and philanthropy were never better joined than through The Nathan Cummings Foundation, whose people believed in these questions and in TPL's willingness and ability to explore them. Without their leadership, this process of understanding simply would not have occurred. Our special thanks go to Charles Halpern, Dick Mark, and Mark Walters.

A deep bow of gratitude is owed now and long into the future to the dozens of authors included in this book who show us a part of their soul through their writings. May a greater fulfilment of our conservation mission be part of our enduring thanks to each of them.

Lastly, without Helen's commitment to her craft, her sense of beauty, and her belief in this project, and without Ann's long understanding and living of these issues and her willingness to explore them with me, this anthology would not sing; it would not even walk.

Thank you.

Peter Forbes
Canaan, N.H.

Preface to the Second Edition

Our Land, Ourselves: Readings on People and Place began as part of a multi-year effort by The Trust for Public Land (TPL) to help itself and the larger conservation movement to more fully understand and apply the core social values imbedded in land conservation. But as we asked ourselves, with the help of the diverse voices collected here, to define the full power of our mission in strengthening communities and fostering a more healthy natural world, we realized the value of extending this discussion to the public at large.

The Trust for Public Land is the only national nonprofit working exclusively to protect land for human enjoyment and well-being. TPL conserves land for recreation and spiritual nourishment and to improve the health and quality of life of American communities. TPL believes that connecting people to land deepens the public's appreciation of nature and their commitment to protect it. Since its founding in 1972, TPL has helped to protect more than one million acres in forty-five states—from expansive recreation areas, to historic homesteads, to pocket-sized city parks—and yet it is time to think beyond numbers of acres saved.

The editors of this anthology believe that the conservation movement stands on the brink of its finest hour, at a time when America needs not only more protected land, but also a strong and clear social promise. With this anthology we hope to kindle many discussions about the connection between land conservation and our yearning, as a culture, for more grounded and purposeful lives. We believe that the collected writings in this anthology can light a path for conservation to grow from technical achievements into a social movement. Second, we have attempted to introduce a variety of voices that demonstrate the vital connection between cultural diversity and biological diversity—how the act of protecting one leads to the health and well being of the other. Lastly, this anthology seeks to offer a contextual significance to land conservation amidst the many pressures in the world today. These writings show that caring for the land goes hand-in-hand with caring for our community and being in service to a larger world. The editors hope that these pages will inform and inspire anyone who thinks about how we might live in a more connected way to our land and to one another.

Peter Forbes
Canaan, N.H.
July 1999

Foreword

It would be difficult to exaggerate the importance of this reader and of the process it launched for The Trust for Public Land, our staff, our supporters, and for the broader land conservation community. In a very real sense we are at a crossroads. The velocity of change in our society is breathtaking, fueled by technological advances in every field and discipline. We are having to react to changes in the structure and substance of our personal and family lives and our workplaces, as well as to dramatic alterations in the landscapes around us.

Not all change is progress. America is losing 7,000 acres daily to development. Most of our wetlands are already lost. The farms and ranches that helped define who we are as a people are being pushed farther and farther out, out of sight and out of mind. Many of our cities and towns lack the green spaces that are the source for physical recreation and spiritual re-creation.

In order to pass onto future generations the special and ordinary places that we need for our physical and spiritual health, we must first help change become progress. Land conservation, like the soil under our feet, must be the bridge between home, good work, meaningful lives, and a hopeful future. We need to view our own good work in the bigger context of being responsible for what actually happens in the world. And to do that we need to harness the power of our relationship with the land and with nature. We must articulate why we feel so passionately about our land and water resources and their importance to our lives.

The conservation of land is one of the most powerful tools for shaping positive change, because it gives communities hope through self-determination. Expanding our cultural understanding of why protecting our land heritage matters to our lives makes us part of a story greater than ourselves. Hope and meaning, together, are the tools that land conservation must use to make an enduring difference. Sharing this understanding with others by telling the stories of how connecting land and people transforms communities has a ripple effect that goes well beyond any individual conservation effort, however large. This reader and the process it launched help us to focus on the "why" of land conservation. These readings help us to guide the values and decisions our communities and society must nurture in order to protect our precious and threatened land. Therein lies the future of land conservation and is what this reader is all about.

I thank the editors of this anthology for their leadership and contribution to the future of our work. I believe that it will have a profound impact on TPL's ability to carry out our land-for-people mission. Lastly, I thank you for your participation and your willingness to help all of us on this earth to better understand and communicate the importance of honoring and protecting our land and water heritage.

> Will Rogers, President
> The Trust for Public Land
> San Francisco, Calif.

Introduction

I spent a fall day ten years ago on my knees working the soil in a vacant lot The Trust for Public Land had just bought on behalf of a local land trust in south Providence, Rhode Island. For most of the morning, I worked silently alongside a Laotian woman my age. We communicated mostly through laughs and nervous exclamations as a truck barreled too close through the narrow streets or when we found a piece of glass or jagged metal buried in the soil. By afternoon, we had cleared almost a quarter acre, and we were comfortable enough with one another for her to try her broken English. Suke was 28, had arrived alone with her two daughters just four months before from a refugee camp on the Thai border, and was waiting for her husband to join her. While she waited, she gardened. Everyday, she walked two miles through a city she didn't know to a place that had become very important to her. At the end of our time together, Suke held my hand for a moment and told me that these urban gardens had made her feel at home in America.

In the years since, I have thought often about Suke. I think about her whenever I consider my own rootlessness, and I am graced by the memory of how quickly she sought land and soil to affirm her place in America. I thought about Suke every time we completed a conservation project, because she asks of me, for whom have we conserved this piece of land? Whose life does this touch?

TPL's good work gave me the experience of Suke, and gave Suke the experience of home. That day was the genesis of this anthology, although it took an intervening ten years in the land trust trenches for me to better understand the great transformative power of land conservation to improve *all* of our lives. The story of Suke, and the stories of many people after her, allowed me to see that this power is possibly the greatest legacy of our good work. Each of us has seen land conservation change a community, has seen the impact far exceed the property boundary, where the resulting alchemy of human cooperation, activism, and the wild has led people to view themselves differently and to live better with one another.

Much of this reader concerns itself with the quest for a new set of ethics around land. Since Aldo Leopold wrote *A Sand County Almanac* in 1949 calling for an American land ethic which might "transform *Homo sapiens* from conqueror of the land-community to plain member and citizen of it," a great deal has happened to elevate that debate. The number of environmental laws has quadrupled and the number of conservation organizations has grown one hundredfold, but economic and social trends suggest that a shared land ethic still eludes us. This reader explores many of the cultural obstacles, but it suggests an additional explanation for our lack of a shared land ethic: the process of land conservation itself. To a large extent, the conservation of land has been disconnected from personal practice and civic behavior.

"Conservation," wrote Leopold, is defined by "a state of harmony between men and nature" which assumes shared values between the two. Values, always intangible, are well described by Wendell Berry as "knowledge, attitudes, and skills; family and community coherence; family and community labor; and cultural or religious principles such as . . .

humility, fidelity, charity, and neighborliness." Leopold was nervous about a form of conservation that was valueless, that "defines no right or wrong, assigns no obligation, calls for no sacrifice, implies no change in the philosophy of values." He was concerned that conservation would become only an outlet for human recreation, as opposed to an inspiration for human re-creation.

The conservation movement has not fully accepted that the root problem spawning its crusade is not loss of species, or decreasing air and water quality, or dwindling wilderness, or even relentless sprawl. These are the symptoms. The root problem is how we humans live each day, and from where we draw our values. Until conservation offers positive alternatives to people about how they might lead their daily lives, a land ethic will elude us.

Mahatma Gandhi, who was largely responsible for leading India's fight for independence and for starting South Africa's successful anti-apartheid movement, spoke about "the dissonance between deed and creed," and how the separation between one's acts and one's ideals led to a fractured individual. In one of history's great connections, Gandhi drew his inspiration for this thinking while in jail in 1908 reading the story of another jailed dissenter, Henry David Thoreau, who had written about fractured people in *Civil Disobedience*.

Thoreau's response to the need for healing in his own life was twofold: to seek nature on the banks of Walden Pond, and to merge his creed and deed to such a point where he was even willing to go to jail for something he believed in. The fact that Thoreau's life story and the stories of his more modern torchbearers such as Helen and Scott Nearing remain such a source of fulfillment and interest is testament to our culture's thirst for what those lives teach us. It is worth pointing out that today we call these people environmentalists but that in their own day they would have called themselves social activists. It is only the modern conservation movement that has separated the imperative of social change from the needs of the earth.

Trying to live by land conservation's example of forbearance and equality may be today's civil disobedience. It may also be exactly what's required to begin to heal the dissonance and contradictions of modern society. Land conservation can help to make people and communities whole.

It is one intent of this anthology to ask its readers to think of land conservation as a form of citizenship. David Suzuki, Canada's leading environmentalist, wrote recently that "consumerism has taken the place of citizenship as the chief way we contribute to the health of our society." Alternatively, the process of saving land takes us out of our private lives to realize something greater for ourselves and our neighbors. It the chance to express our allegiance to ideals, to one another, and to the land, thereby enabling each one of us to a become citizen of a specific place. More emphatic and political than a sense of place, the act of land conservation offers us the choice of place. To say "this is my home and I care about it enough to protect it" is the essence of citizenship, and to act on such words begins to move us from isolation to community.

We have tried to present this anthology in a logical manner, by stating the challenges, reviewing the obstacles, and outlining the possible solutions. Nonetheless, to our reader, our linear goals may appear to have been thwarted by the interconnectedness of each idea to the next. Herein lies the theme. "Wholism" is one of the essential truths of a land ethic. Like the natural world, the ideas in this reader are all related in overlapping layers of understanding and meaning. How we live in the world, our security, our health and our happiness, influence how the world is. Conversely, the quality of our natural world is the quality of our being. What we do to it is ultimately what we do to ourselves.

This volume, *Our Land, Ourselves: Readings on People and Place,* is the garden of questions that grew from that one seed planted by Suke in a vacant lot she came to call home. We have sought more to raise questions than to provide answers. This is an exploration of values, not a conclusive statement about them. The volume, itself, is not meant to be complete. It is offered to everyone as a starting point in what we hope will be a long and fruitful discussion in our communities about conservation, ethics, and the meaning of our work. We hope these readings inspire new ideas and crystalize old ones. And so, this volume is like a question mark, asking a heartfelt consideration and trusting the response.

Peter Forbes
Canaan, N.H.

I : OUR CHALLENGE

Chapter 1: Does Land Conservation Matter?

We begin by offering different perspectives on what constitutes the greatest aspirations of land conservation. Ultimately, these readings ask us to consider in what service can conservation be most relevant today. These readings ask us why and for whom are we saving land, and what difference our work makes in addressing the problems of the day: rootlessness, overconsumption, and decaying social fabric. The readings suggest how conservation can teach values such as forbearance and limitation, equality and service, celebration of life and generational responsibility. Conservation can offer an important cultural counterpoint to other prevailing forces in our society by giving people a connection to a story greater than themselves, one grounded in nature, history, and community. Why does land matter to us and why should we work to save it?

→>-<+

"Scarcely any human being wholly escapes the yearning to know truth, to understand life and events. Men commune with nature —with sunshine, the stars, the birds, flowers, the wind, the showers, the trees and rivers, the plains, the forests, the mountain chains. From this communion they draw inspiration."

—Scott Nearing, *Where Is Civilization Going?*

→>-<+

ALDO LEOPOLD
A Sand County Almanac · *1949*

All ethics so far evolved rest upon a single premise: that the individual is a member of a community of interdependent parts. His instincts prompt him to compete for his place in the community, but his ethics prompt him also to co-operate (perhaps in order that there may be a place to compete for).

The land ethic simply enlarges the boundaries of the community to include soils, waters, plants, and animals, or collectively: the land.

This sounds simple: do we not already sing our love for and obligation to the land of the free and the home of the brave? Yes, but just what and whom do we love? Certainly not the soil, which we are sending helter-skelter downriver. Certainly not the waters, which we assume have no function except to turn turbines, float barges, and carry off sewage. Certainly not the plants, of which we exterminate whole communities without batting an eye. Certainly not the animals, of which we have already extirpated many of the largest and most beautiful species. A land ethic of course cannot prevent the alteration, management, and use of these "resources," but it does affirm their right to continued existence, and, at least in spots, their continued existence in a natural state.

In short, a land ethic changes the role of *Homo sapiens* from conqueror of the land-community to plain member and citizen of it. It implies respect for his fellow-members, and also respect for the community as such.

In human history, we have learned (I hope) that the conqueror role is eventually self-defeating. Why? Because it is implicit in such a role that the conqueror knows, *ex cathedra*, just what makes the community clock tick, and just what and who is valuable, and what and who is worthless, in community life. It always turns out that he knows neither, and this is why his conquests eventually defeat themselves.

In the biotic community, a parallel situation exists. Abraham knew exactly what the land was for: it was to drip milk and honey into Abraham's mouth. At the present moment, the assurance with which we regard this assumption is inverse to the degree of our education.

The ordinary citizen today assumes that science knows what makes the community clock tick; the scientist is equally sure that he does not. He knows that the biotic mechanism is so complex that its workings may never be fully understood.

That man is, in fact, only a member of a biotic team is shown by an ecological interpretation of history. Many historical events, hitherto explained solely in terms of human enterprise, were actually biotic interactions between people and land. The characteristics of the land determined the facts quite as potently as the characteristics of the men who lived on it. [. . .]

No important change in ethics was ever accomplished without an internal change in our intellectual emphases, loyalties, affections, and convictions. The proof that conservation has not yet touched these foundations of conduct lies in the fact that philosophy and religion have not yet heard of it. In our attempt to make conservation easy, we have made it trivial. [. . .]

It is inconceivable to me that an ethical relation to land can exist without love, respect, and admiration for land, and a high regard for its value. By value, I of course mean something far broader than mere economic value; I mean value in the philosophical sense.

Perhaps the most serious obstacle impeding the evolution of a land ethic is the fact that our educational and economic system is headed away from, rather than toward, an intense consciousness of land. Your true modern is separated from the land by many middlemen, and by innumerable physical gadgets. He has no vital relation to it; to him it is the space between cities on which crops grow. Turn him loose for a day on the land, and if the spot does not happen to be a golf links or a "scenic" area, he is bored stiff. If crops could be raised by hydroponics instead of farming, it would suit him very well. Synthetic substitutes for wood, leather, wool, and other natural land products suit him better than the originals. In short, land is something he has "outgrown."

Almost equally serious as an obstacle to a land ethic is the attitude of the farmer for whom the land is still an adversary, or a taskmaster that keeps him in slavery. Theoretically, the mechanization of farming ought to cut the farmer's chains, but whether it really does is debatable.

One of the requisites for an ecological comprehension of land is an understanding of ecology, and this is by no means coextensive with "education"; in fact, much higher education seems deliberately to avoid ecological concepts. An understanding of ecology does not necessarily originate in courses bearing ecological labels; it is quite as likely to be labeled geography, botany, agronomy, history, or economics. This is as it should be, but whatever the label, ecological training is scarce.

The case for a land ethic would appear hopeless but for the minority which is in obvious revolt against these "modern" trends.

The "key-log" which must be moved to release the evolutionary process for an ethic is simply this: quit thinking about decent land-use as solely an economic problem. Examine each question in terms of what is ethically and esthetically right, as well as what is economically expedient. A thing is right when it tends to preserve the integrity, stability, and beauty of the biotic community. It is wrong when it tends otherwise.

It of course goes without saying that economic feasibility limits the tether of what can or cannot be done for land. It always has and it always will. The fallacy the economic determinists have tied around our collective neck, and which we now need to cast off, is the belief that economics determines *all* land-use. This is simply not true. An innumerable host of actions and attitudes, comprising perhaps the bulk of all land relations, is determined by the land-user's tastes and predilections, rather than by his purse. The bulk of all land relations hinges on investments of time, forethought, skill, and faith rather than on investments of cash. As a land-user thinketh, so is he.

I have purposely presented the land ethic as a product of social evolution because nothing so important as an ethic is ever "written." Only the most superficial student of history supposes that Moses "wrote" the Decalogue; it evolved in the minds of a thinking community, and Moses wrote a tentative summary of it for a "seminar." I say tentative because evolution never stops.

The evolution of a land ethic is an intellectual as well as emotional process. Conservation is paved with good intentions which prove to be futile, or even dangerous, because they are devoid of critical understanding either of the land, or of economic land-use. I think it is a truism that as the ethical frontier advances from the individual to the community, its intellectual content increases.

→>◄-

Jean Giono
The Man Who Planted Trees · *1954*

[*Editor's note:* This passage from *The Man Who Planted Trees* tells of the narrator's encounter, in 1920, with Elzeard Bouffier, a French peasant who was single-handedly reforesting the war-ravaged hills around his village in southern France. Giono's fable has inspired many tree-planting efforts around the world.] The oaks of 1910 were then ten years old and taller than either of us. It was an impressive spectacle. I was literally speechless and, as he did not talk, we spent the whole day walking in silence through his forest. In three sections, it measured eleven kilometers in length and three kilometers at its greatest width. Then you remembered that all this had sprung from the hands and the soul of this one man, without technical resources, you understood that men could be as effectual as God in other realms than that of destruction.

He had pursued his plan, and beech trees as high as my shoulder, spreading out as far as the eye could reach, confirmed it. He showed me handsome clumps of birch planted five years before—that is, in 1915, when I had been fighting at Verdun. He had set them out in all the valleys where he had guessed—and rightly—that there was moisture almost at the surface of the ground. They were as delicate as young girls and very well established.

Creation seemed to come about in a sort of chain reaction. He did not worry about it; he was determinedly pursuing his task in all its simplicity; but as we went back toward the village I saw water flowing in brooks that had been dry since the memory of man. This was the most impressive result of chain reaction that I had seen. These dry streams had once, long ago, run with water. Some of the dreary villages I mentioned before had been built on the sites of ancient Roman settlements, traces of which still remained; and archæologists, exploring there, had found fishhooks where, in the twentieth century, cisterns were needed to assure a small supply of water.

The wind, too, scattered seeds. As the water reappeared, so there reappeared willows, rushes, meadows, gardens, flowers, and a certain purpose in being alive. But the transformation took place so gradually that it became part of the pattern without causing any astonishment. Hunters, climbing into the wilderness in pursuit of hares or wild boar, had of course noticed the sudden growth of little trees, but had attributed it to some natural caprice of the earth. That is why no one meddled with Elzéard Bouffier's work. If he had been detected he would have had opposition. He was indetectable. Who in the villages or in the administration could have dreamed of such perseverance in a magnificent generosity?

→►◄←

"There was an 87-year hiatus from the Declaration of Independence to the Emancipation Proclamation and the freeing of American blacks from slavery . . . the idea of an inalienable right of self-determination has moved with irresistible force to become what Jefferson claimed it was in 1776: a self-evident truth. It is now nature's turn to be liberated."

—Donald Worster, *The Wilderness of History*

→►◄←

Wendell Berry
A Native Hill · 1969

Sometimes I can no longer think in the house or in the garden or in the cleared fields. They bear too much resemblance to our failed human history—failed, because it has led to this human present that is such a bitterness and a trial. And so I go to the woods. As I go in under the trees, dependably, almost at once, and by nothing I do, things fall into place. I enter an order that does not exist outside, in the human spaces. I feel my life take its place among the lives—the trees, the annual plants, the animals and birds, the living of all these and the dead—that go and have gone to make the life of the earth. I am less important than I thought, the human race is less important than I thought. I rejoice in that. My mind loses its urgings, senses its nature, and is free. The forest grew here in its own time, and so I will live, suffer and rejoice, and die in my own time. There is nothing that I may decently hope for that I cannot reach by patience as well as by anxiety. The hill, which is a part of America, has killed no one in the service of the American government.

Then why should I, who am a fragment of the hill? I wish to be as peaceable as my land, which does no violence, though it has been the scene of violence and has had violence done to it.

How, having a consciousness, an intelligence, a human spirit —all the vaunted equipment of my race—can I humble myself before a mere piece of the earth and speak of myself as its fragment? Because my mind transcends the hill only to be filled with it, to comprehend it a little, to know that it lives on the hill in time as well as in place, to recognize itself as the hill's fragment.

The false and truly belittling transcendence is ownership. The hill has had more owners than its owners have had years— they are grist for its mill. It has had few friends. But I wish to be its friend, for I think it serves its friends well. It tells them they are fragments of its life. In its life they transcend their years.

→>—<←

"The more we come to dwell in an explained world, a world of uniformity and regularity, world without possibility of miracles, the less we are able to encounter anything but ourselves."

—NEIL EVERDEN, *The Social Creation of Nature*

→>—<←

GARY SNYDER
The Place, The Region, and The Commons · 1990

We need to make a world-scale "Natural Contract" with the oceans, the air, the birds in the sky. The challenge is to bring the whole victimized world of "common pool resources" into the Mind of the Commons. As it stands now, any resource on earth that is not nailed down will be seen as fair game to the timber buyers or petroleum geologists from Osaka, Rotterdam, or Boston. The pressures of growing populations and the powers of entrenched (but fragile, confused, and essentially leaderless) economic systems warp the likelihood of any of us seeing clearly. Our perception of how entrenched they are may also be something of a delusion.

Sometimes it seems unlikely that a society as a whole can make wise choices. Yet there is no choice but to call for the "recovery of the commons"—and this in a modern world which doesn't quite realize what it has lost. Take back, like the night, that which is shared by all of us, that which is our larger being. There will be no "tragedy of the commons" greater than this: if we do not recover the commons—regain personal, local, community, and people's direct involvement in sharing (in *being*) the web of the wild world—that world will keep slipping away. Eventually our complicated industrial capitalist/socialist mixes will bring down much of the living system that supports us. And, it is clear, the loss of a local commons heralds the end of self-sufficiency and signals the doom of the vernacular culture of the region. This is still happening in the far corners of the world.

The commons is a curious and elegant social institution within which human beings once lived free political lives while weaving through natural systems. The commons is a level of organization of human society that includes the nonhuman. The level above the local commons is the bioregion. Understanding the commons and its role within the larger regional culture is one more step toward integrating ecology with economy.

RODERICK NASH
The Rights of Nature · *1989*

The comparison of those who liberated slaves over a century ago to those who would liberate nature today is at once encouraging and disturbing. On the one hand it might be heartening for the new animal rightists and biocentrists to remember that civil war and the abolition of slavery seemed just as unlikely in the 1830s as implementation of their moral ideals does a century and a half later. The abolitionists initially faced a culture united in the consensus that right and wrong did not apply to relations with slaves any more than they did to relations with cows or bacteria or rivers. The full weight of private property supported the slaveholders' cause, just as it does that of contemporary owners of nature. The ethical community ended then at the line between white and black; now it ends, for many, at the human-nature boundary. William Lloyd Garrison fully expected himself and his colleagues to be "ridiculed as fools, scorned as visionaries, branded as disorganizers, reviled as madmen, threatened and perhaps punished as traitors." But, Garrison added, "we shall bide our time." He proved as patient as he was committed. In 1829, at the beginning of his abolitionist career, he characterized the established ethical system as higher than the Alps and spoke of the necessity of dismantling it "brick by brick, and foot by foot, till it is reduced so low that it may be overturned without burying the nation in its ruins." Garrison knew the length of time this might require. He understood in the 1830s that "the philanthropists who are now pleading in behalf of the oppressed may not live to witness the dawn which will precede the glorious day of universal emancipation." Yet agitation continued and gradually the majority in the North came to accept the abolitionists' principal contention that slavery was incompatible with the American liberal tradition. Garrison did live to witness the end of slavery and the inclusion, at least by law, of all blacks in an extended ethical community. The price, to be sure, was high: four years of civil war and a loss of nearly a million human lives.

The chances of this process recurring on behalf of other species and nature itself seems to some as remote today as freedom for slaves did in the early nineteenth century. But some advocates of animals and nature don't agree: "The animal rights issue," notes Henry Holzer, "is at the same place now as the slavery issue was fifty years before Abolition." In fact, most of the ingredients that sparked the Civil War presently exist. There is what many construe to be the denial of natural rights to exploited and oppressed members of the American ecological community. Ownership, what some even call the enslavement of nonhuman species and of the environment, is again the explosive issue. In the last two decades advocates of environmental ethics just as earnest as Garrison and as impassioned as Stowe have appeared. They have found their Thomas Jefferson in Aldo Leopold and their John Brown in Dave Foreman. Some are already acting on their ethical convictions. Radical environmentalism has produced both civil disobedience and violent resistance. As a spokesperson for the Animal Liberation Front declared, "It's like the Underground Railroad and slavery . . . sometimes people have to go outside the law to save lives. Any movement for social change has required disobedience." An Earth First! publication of 1987 similarly noted that the "'Underground Railroad' was destructive of the private economic concerns of those who saw the slave as just another exploitable resource." The writer pointed out that disobedience was necessary when British administrators "refused to negotiate with radical colonists whom [they] associated with numerous attacks on public and private property." The upshot was the Boston Tea Party and eventually the American Revolution, because "the sluggish minds of men in government failed to acknowledge the changing times."

+>-<+

WALLACE STEGNER
Marking the Sparrow's Fall · *1998*

Are we any closer than we were in 1949 to a land ethic as widely acknowledged (however widely evaded) as our commitment to civil rights? Or have we, indulging habits learned on our careless frontiers and given continuing force by the Reagan administration, pushed closer to the showdown that, if not so dramatic and totally annihilating as the atomic showdown we simultaneously risk, will surely bring a sharp decline in the quality of American life?

Certain inescapable facts are relevant. At mid-century the population of the United States was 150 million. Since then we have added more people than the whole country contained in 1900, and now number above 230 million. That 53 percent growth above the 1950 base has meant what we in our lives are witnessing: more mouths to feed, a greater and greater demand for energy to run our industries and our homes, more digging for minerals and coal, more cutting of timber, more drilling for oil on- and off-shore, more automobiles to carry us around and foul the air, more paving-over of land for freeways, roads, driveways, parking areas, and tennis courts, more orchards and fields gone into subdivisions or industrial plants or shopping centers, more bombing and missile ranges in the deserts, more ski resorts in the mountains, more smokestacks and acid rain, more Love Canals and toxic waste sites and more dirty politics to cover them up, less green, less space, less freedom, less health, more intensive working of the soils still left in agriculture, a longer and longer stretching of a rubber band not indefinitely stretchable, a temporarily more comfortable, ultimately less plentiful, increasingly less spiritually rewarding life. ·

Precisely because we could not ignore the symptoms, we managed some corrections, especially during the 1960s and 1970s, before the Reagan administration undertook to dismantle the gains. Most of the corrections we measure by federal laws; and though Leopold himself warned us against expecting the government to exercise our conscience for us, we would be in infinitely worse shape without the Clean Air Act, the Clean Water Act, the Strip Mining Act, the Wilderness Act, the Federal Land Policy and Management Act (FLPMA), the Land and Water Conservation Fund Act, the Alaska National Interest Lands Conservation Act (ANILCA), and many other laws that have been enacted since Leopold wrote. [. . .]

That old party of loyalists has been immensely augmented in the past twenty years as people began to protest dirty air, poisoned water, and creeping uglification. But how much evidence is there that a real conversion has taken place in a substantial part of the public? Earth Year fired up the college campuses briefly and subsided to something less than a conflagration. Is there anything to the environmental movement now besides the activity of those irreconcilable "environmental extremists" who so exasperated and frustrated Mr. Watt? Is environmentalism any more than the effort of a comfortable middle class to preserve its amenities? Do workers share in it? Blacks? Chicanos? College students? The young? The old? Is there perhaps even a backlash against environmentalism? [. . .]

People had every reason to turn pale, hide, flee, in the spring of 1969. But they hid or fled from the shadow of a fear, not from the true substance of their danger. From the thing that should have terrified them there is no hiding. How do we flee from ourselves, from our incontinent fertility, our wastes and poisons, the industrial society in which we are guilty, suffering participants?

Some years ago Stewart L. Udall, then Secretary of the Interior, published a book summarizing the history of land use and abuse in the United States and suggesting a "land ethic" by which we might be guided. He called his book *The Quiet Crisis;* most readers probably read "quiet" as also meaning "slow," "delayed." Many probably assumed that he was talking primarily about open space and scenic beauty. To the average city dweller of the early 1960s—and more and more we all tend to be city dwellers—such concerns probably seemed minor by comparison with the cold war, the bomb, racial strife, inflation, the disintegrating cities, and much else. To people living in the ghetto these matters may have seemed, and may still seem, frivolous.

They were not frivolous—that was Mr. Udall's point. Neither were they limited to open space and scenic beauty. Neither have they remained quiet. While we watched the horizon for mushroom clouds, a funnel-shaped one came up behind us with terrifying swiftness. It is perfectly clear now that we can destroy ourselves quite as completely, if not quite so spectacularly, through continuing abuse of our environment as we can through some mad or vengeful or preventive finger on the atomic trigger. Conservation still properly concerns itself with national parks and wildernesses, but it has not for some years been confined to them. As Mr. Udall says in another context, true conservation begins wherever people are and with whatever trouble they are in.

People are everywhere, and in trouble wherever they are. It is not only amenity, not only quality of living, not only a supply of raw materials or open space for our grandchildren, that we must fight for. Paul B. Sears and William Vogt and others told us what was at stake sixty-odd years ago in the Dust Bowl years: survival. It is even more at stake now—survival of this civilization, perhaps even survival of the living world. And it is later than we think.

→>--<-

"We are finally coming to recognize that the natural environment is the exploited proletariat, the downtrodden nigger of everybody's industrial system. [. . .] Nature must also have its natural rights."

—Theodore Roszak

STEPHEN R. KELLERT
Kinship to Mastery · 1997

A world devoid of natural symbolism would be a world of emotionally and mentally stunted people. A society reliant solely on artificial creation would strike us as not only odd but oppressive. Our current anxiety about the diminished state of civil discourse and the intellectual sterility of the mass media perhaps reflects this growing concern. Children's books increasingly lack the emotional power of many traditional stories, few modern politicians seem to possess the rhetorical power of a Julius Caesar or a Winston Churchill, and the level of everyday conversation seems coarser and ever more inarticulate. An impoverished relation between people and nature may underlie this decline in imagery and effective rhetoric. Environmental destruction produces not only material injury but also a wounded intellectual and communicative capacity. [. . .]

People also derive advantage from recognizing an underlying order binding humans with the natural world. We reap personal faith and confidence in believing that life possesses intrinsic meaning, value, and purpose. This conviction imbues in us the calming assurance that the world is fundamentally good, harmonious, worthwhile.

These beliefs can become particularly sustaining in times of crisis and adversity. A feeling of profound connection with nature offers a sense of relationship and enduring value in the face of individual separation and aloneness. We derive faith and optimism from our belief in a unity that transcends our lone and often vulnerable selves. This commitment musters in us the will to persevere in the face of setbacks. By connecting with the rest of creation, we find the trials of life somehow less overwhelming. This wisdom can be fathomed in an Ojibway expression: "Sometimes I go about pitying myself, and all the time I am being carried on great winds across the sky."

—→—←—

"Recreational development is a job not of building roads into lovely country, but of building receptivity into the still unlovely human mind."

—ALDO LEOPOLD, *A Sand County Almanac*

—→—←—

PENNY NEWMAN
Killing Legally with Toxic Waste · 1994

Twenty years ago, George Wiley, an American civil rights leader, told the crowd at Harvard University's Earth Day rally:

> I'd like to share with you some concerns that I have about the movement around the environment. . . . If you are a serious movement, you must be prepared to take on the giant corporations who are the primary polluters and perpetrators of some of the worst conditions that affect the environment of the country and indeed the world . . . [but] it has been my experience that most of you aren't going to deal with the problem at the level that it is going to help the welfare recipient, the poor

person in the ghettos and the barrios. Most of you are not even going to listen to the voices coming from those communities. You won't ask what they want, and how they want to deal with the problems of their environment, or indeed whether they want to deal with the problems of environment at all—because they feel there are other more pressing priorities in their lives.

The environmental movement in the United States did not heed those words. Instead it excluded from the decision-making process large segments of the population, usually those most directly and severely affected. In its isolation it defined the problem, segregated issues, outlined the agenda and identified "solutions." That these ignored women, children and the poor should not be surprising.

Mainstream environmental organizations from the Sierra Club to the World Wildlife Fund and Environmental Defense Fund have become part of "the system" where being "reasonable" is the driving force, and there is little consideration of the impact on people. These organizations are staffed primarily by scientists, lawyers, economists and political lobbyists. Although many may have an adversarial relationship with agencies such as the EPA, their differences are frequently of degree rather than substance, with an emphasis on tightening or enforcing existing laws rather than developing new approaches. The short-sightedness of these environmental groups, in being concerned with "controlling" rather than "preventing" pollution, has encouraged the earth's continued destruction.

These groups have failed also to understand how various

issues, such as ozone depletion, acid rain, toxic wastes, and harmful pesticides, are interconnected and are really manifestations of a single, larger issue—the massive production of man-made chemicals by the petrochemical industry. That failure has led to our inability even to begin to address the real problem and to find real solutions. By avoiding identifying the larger issue as the underlying cause of each of the various environmental hazards, we continue to respond in a crisis mentality, bouncing from one trendy issue to the next.

My plea [. . .] is to put wilderness protection (and its radical edge, deep ecology) in its place, to recognize it as a distinctively North Atlantic brand of environmentalism, whose export and expansion must be done with caution, care, and above all, with humility. For in the poor and heavily populated countries of the South, protected areas cannot be managed with guns and guards but must, rather, be managed with full cognizance of the rights of the people who lived in (and oftentimes cared for) the forest before it became a national park or a world heritage site. [. . .]

For to the Costa Rican peasant, the Ecuadorian fisherman, the Indonesian tribal, or the slum dweller in Bombay, wilderness preservation can hardly be more "deep" than pollution control, energy conservation, ecological urban planning, or sustainable agriculture.

—RAMACHANDRA GUHA, *Deep Ecology Revisited*

Chapter 2: A Rolling Stone Gathers No Moss

This chapter presents the economic and cultural barriers to an enduring land ethic in America. Conservation, for it to matter, cannot fight battles without first being sure of the nature of the larger war. It must directly confront the society in which it is based if it hopes to address root problems, as opposed to just symptoms. The voices in this chapter suggest the degree to which we have become a culture driven by self-preservation, market efficiencies, global economics, and the delusion of no limits. "Interest-based" values are quickly replacing "land-based" values such as mutual aid, interdependence, and connection to a larger story.

If we define our mission as being the creation of a land ethic, how do we most effectively pit our values against the predominant values of the day? How can "sense of place" be maintained in our technological age with its forces toward growth, transience, and community fracture? What is the impact on humans of living in an insulated way rather than an integrated way? How does being divorced from what feeds us, clothes us, and shelters us impact our lives?

+>-<+

JAMES HOWARD KUNSTLER
The Geography of Nowhere · 1993

Thirty years ago, Lewis Mumford said of post–World War II development, "the end product is an encapsulated life, spent more and more either in a motor car or within the cabin of darkness before a television set." The whole wicked, sprawling, megalopolitan mess, he gloomily predicted, would completely demoralize mankind and lead to nuclear holocaust.

It hasn't come to that, but what Mumford deplored was just the beginning of a process that, instead of blowing up the world, has nearly wrecked the human habitat in America. Ever-busy, ever-building, ever-in-motion, ever-throwing-out the old for the new, we have hardly paused to think about what we are so busy building, and what we have thrown away. Meanwhile, the everyday landscape becomes more nightmarish and unmanageable each year. For many, the word *development* itself has become a dirty word.

Eighty percent of everything ever built in America has been built in the last fifty years, and most of it is depressing, brutal, ugly, unhealthy, and spiritually degrading—the jive-plastic commuter tract home wastelands, the Potemkin village shopping plazas with their vast parking lagoons, the Lego-block hotel complexes, the "gourmet mansardic" junk-food joints, the Orwellian office "parks" featuring buildings sheathed in the same reflective glass as the sunglasses worn by chain-gang guards, the particle-board garden apartments rising up in every meadow and cornfield, the freeway loops around every big and little city with their clusters of discount merchandise marts, the whole destructive, wasteful, toxic, agoraphobia-inducing spectacle that politicians proudly call "growth."

The newspaper headlines may shout about global warming, extinctions of living species, the devastation of rain forests, and other worldwide catastrophes, but Americans evince a striking complacency when it comes to their everyday environment and the growing calamity that it represents.

I had a hunch that many other people find their surroundings as distressing as I do my own, yet I sensed too that they lack the vocabulary to understand what is wrong with the places they ought to know best.

→>-<←

JAMES HILLMAN
Inter Views · *1983*

[*Editor's note: Anima mundi* describes the belief that our souls are not just within us but also in nature and in the world, and that damage done to the world is damage done to our souls.]

Let's take a husband and wife in a modern suburb, and they fight about drink and money and in-laws and love and little habits. Then he goes to analysis and she goes to analysis and they work on the relationship, and they are good sincere patients who try—group therapy, team or office therapy, family therapy, sex therapy—they get it all together as human decent people. They may even go to Church. And still there is a terrible misery going on, because the room in which they're set, its low ceiling, thin hollow doors, the bed, the dishes, the TV programs, the magazines, the light tubes, the furniture they have around them, and so on and so on, the whole world of material things, verbal things, institutional things in which their marriage is set is nasty, brutish, ugly, cheap, shoddy, vicious— without soul at all. Fake. How can they possibly straighten out their situation if the whole stage set including the lines in the script are fake?

Wait—let me go on: Psychotherapy is something very strange in a world like this. It used to rely on a bourgeois world that had certain values and kinds of things, qualities, that had to be seen through, with irony, with skepsis. See the repressed. But that world has disappeared. The politics, language, education, institutions that upheld the marriage disappeared, the buildings, streets, lights, food, words, tables and chairs are gone: but psychotherapy still works as if all that scenery is still around, analyzing the marriage with theories of 1920 in a 1980 set. Unless psychotherapy takes into account the sickness of the world, it can never really work, because the *anima mundi* is sick now. Pathology is "out there." You feel it on the highway, you feel it in the car, you feel it in your sense that something is out of tune, false or ugly or unemotional or without soul or vapid or sexless, tasteless. How can psychoanalysis justify itself, two people in a room talking?

+>-<+

BRIAN SWIMME
Hidden Heart of the Cosmos · 1996

Where are we initiated into the universe? To answer we need to reflect on what our children experience over and over again, at night, in a setting similar to those children in the past who gathered in the caves and listened to the chant of the elders. If we think in terms of pure quantities of time the answer is immediate: the cave has been replaced with the television room and the chant with the advertisement. One could say that the chant has been replaced with the television *show*, but at the core of each show, driving the action, and determining whether or not the show will survive the season, is the advertisement. That is the essential message that will be there night after night and season after season. Television's *Bonanza, Cheers,* and *Cosby* shows all come and go; the advertisement endures through every change.

What is the effect on our children? Before a child enters first grade science class, and before entering in any real way into our religious ceremonies, a child will have soaked in thirty thousand advertisements. The time our teenagers spend absorbing ads is more than their total stay in high school. None of us feels very good about this, but for the most part we just ignore it. It's background. It's just there, part of what's going on. We learned to accept it so long ago we hardly ever think about it anymore.

But imagine how different we would feel if we heard about a country that programmed its citizenry in its religious dogmas in such a manner. In fact, it was just such accounts concerning the leaders of the former Soviet Union that outraged us for decades, the thought that they would take young children and subject them to brainwashing in Soviet lies, removing their natural feelings for their parents or for God or for the truth of history, and replacing these with the assumptions necessary for their dictatorship to continue its oppressive domination.

Immersed in the religion of consumerism, we are unable to take such comparisons seriously. We tell ourselves soothing clichés, such as the obvious fact that television ads are not put on by any political dictatorship. We tell ourselves that ads are simply the efforts of our corporations to get us interested in their various products. But as with any reality that we rarely pay any serious attention to, there may be a lot more going on there than we are aware of. Just the sheer amount of time we spend in the world of the ad suggests we might well devote a moment to examining that world more carefully.

The advertisers of course are not some bad persons with evil designs. They're just doing their job. On the other hand, we can also say that their primary concern is not explicitly the well-being of our children. Why should it be? Their objective is to create ads that are successful for their company, and this means to get the television viewer interested in their product. But already we can see that this is a less than desirable situation. After all, we parents demand that our children's teachers, to take just one example, should have our children's best interests foremost in mind. Such teachers will shape our children when they are young and vulnerable, so of course we want this shaping to be done only by people who care. So to hand over so much of our children's young lives to people who obviously do not have our children's well-being foremost in mind is at the very least questionable.

But at a deeper level, what we need to confront is the power of the advertiser to promulgate a world-view, a mini-cosmology, that is based upon dissatisfaction and craving.

One of the clichés for how to construct an ad captures the point succinctly: "An ad's job is to make them unhappy with what they have."

We rarely think of ads as being shaped by explicit world-views, and that precisely is why they are so effective. The last thing we want to think about as we're lying on the couch relaxing is the philosophy behind the ad. So as we soak it all up, it sinks down deep in our psyche. And if this takes place in the adult soul, imagine how much more damage is done in the psyches of our children, which have none of our protective cynicisms but which draw in the ad's imagery and message as if they were coming from a trusted parent or teacher.

Advertisers in the corporate world are of course offered lucrative recompense, and, with that financial draw, our corporations attract humans from the highest strata of IQs. And our best artistic talent. And any sports hero or movie star they want to buy. Combining so much brain power and social status with sophisticated electronic graphics and the most penetrating psychological techniques, these teams of highly intelligent adults descend upon all of us, even upon children not yet in school, with the simple desire to create in us a dissatisfaction for our lives and a craving for yet another consumer product. It's hard to imagine any child having the capacities necessary to survive such a lopsided contest, especially when it's carried out ten thousand times a year, with no cultural condom capable of blocking out the consumerism virus. Could even one child in the whole world endure that onslaught and come out intact? Extremely doubtful. Put it all together and you can see why it's no great mystery that consumerism has become the dominant world faith of every continent of the planet today.

The point I wish to make is not just that our children are such easy prey. It's not just that the rushing river of advertisements determines the sorts of shoes our children desire, the sorts of clothes and toys and games and sugar cereals that they must have. It's not just the unhappiness they are left with whenever they cannot have such commodities, an unhappiness that in many cases leads to aggressive violence of the worst kinds in order to obtain by force what their parents will not or cannot give them. All of this is of great concern, but the point I wish to focus on here has to do with the question of how we are initiated into a world.

Advertisements are where our children receive their cosmology, their basic grasp of the world's meaning, which amounts to their primary religious faith, though unrecognized as such. I use the word "faith" here to mean cosmology on the personal level. Faith is that which a person holds to be the hard-boiled truth about reality. The advertisement is our culture's primary vehicle for providing our children with their personal cosmologies. As this awful fact sinks into awareness, the first healthy response is one of denial. It is just too horrible to think that we live in a culture that has replaced authentic spiritual development with the advertisement's crass materialism. And yet when one compares the pitiful efforts we employ for moral development with the colossal and frenzied energies we pour into advertising, it is like comparing a high school football game with World War II. Nothing that happens in one hour on the weekend makes the slightest dent in the strategic bombing taking place day and night fifty-two weeks of the year.

Perhaps the more recalcitrant children will require upward of a hundred thousand ads before they cave in and accept consumerism's basic world-view. But eventually we all get the message. It's a simple cosmology, told with great effect and delivered a billion times each day not only to Americans of course but to nearly everyone in the planetary reach of the ad: *humans exist to work at jobs, to earn money, to get stuff.* The image of the ideal human is also deeply set in our minds by the unending preachments of the ad. The ideal is not Jesus or

Socrates. Forget all about Rachel Carson or Confucius or Martin Luther King, Jr., and all their suffering and love and wisdom. In the propaganda of the ad the ideal people, the fully human humans, are relaxed and carefree—drinking Pepsis around a pool—unencumbered by powerful ideas concerning the nature of goodness, undisturbed by visions of suffering that could be alleviated if humans were committed to justice. None of that ever appears. In the religion of the ad the task of civilization is much simpler. The ultimate meaning for human existence is getting all this stuff. That's paradise. And the meaning of the Earth? Premanufactured consumer stuff.

+>−<+

EVAN EISENBERG
The Ecology of Eden · 1998

Like our living allies, machines coevolve with us. They shape our evolution, both cultural and biological, almost as thoroughly as we shape theirs. We think we control them; in truth, they have a life and a logic of their own. As in the case of our living allies, there is a great deal going on that we do not fully control or comprehend.

Our incomprehension is, as usual, most striking in the realm of ecology. To speak of "the machine in the garden" is misleading, for the machine is never just *in* the garden. Machines are not just superimposed on ecosystems; they displace old ecosystems and create new ones, in which they are often the dominant species. They set up new energy flows. They reweave the food web. Cars are the most glaring example, but there are many others. The lawn mower is a noisy grazing animal that has coevolved with a very small group of perennial grasses (a simpler pasture than any other grazing animal encourages); together they suppress the complex plant and animal communities that would otherwise claim that turf. The tractor is a huge animal that spurs the growth of opportunistic annual grasses while alternately flattening and upending the home of the soil population.

As with our living allies, some machines are not really allies at all, merely hangers-on. Video games, motor yachts, leaf-blowers, and about half the items in the Hammacher Schlemmer catalogue are the rats and pigeons of the machine world, nibbling at our energy supplies without offering much in return. Television sets are perhaps the cleverest parasites, since they encourage humans to multiply all kinds of machines, from assault rifles to television sets.

To describe machines as if they were alive is a conceit, but a useful one. It reminds us to keep an eye on them. For they are not simply tools that lie inert in our hands, but active members of ecological associations whose effects we have not yet learned to gauge. [. . .]

At the turn of this century, America was the paradise of public transportation, with the best and best-ridden network in the world. Each railroad suburb was effectively a village, clustered within walking distance of its station, with plenty of healthy countryside between one suburb and the next—a happy artifact of the steam engine, which was hard to start and stop. The electric streetcar made a closer spacing possible, and (as Sam

Bass Warner has shown) began the process of sprawl; yet if cities trebled in size, they remained recognizably cities. At the nexus of the web, the city's business district remained healthy.

Two decades later, the web was ripped to shreds, largely by one man. Henry Ford had promised to "build a motor car for the great multitude," so that every man might "enjoy with his family the blessings of hours of pleasure in God's great open spaces." In 1908, he made good on that promise by launching the Model T, the first mass-produced automobile.

If in 1905 you had tried to fit all Americans into the existing fleet of registered passenger cars, 1,078 would have had to squeeze into each. In 1920, only 13 would have had to share each car—unsafe, but not inconceivable. In the same year, the figure for the United Kingdom was 228; for France, 247; for Germany, 1,017.

All over America, a black carpet was rolled out for the newcomer. Automakers, tire-makers, oil companies, road contractors, and developers joined in lobbying for new roads, which were promptly built at public expense. While streets and cars were heavily subsidized, streetcars were left to the mercies of the "free market." Most streetcar companies had signed agreements in the 1890s guaranteeing a five-cent fare; though unlooked-for inflation (fed by new Alaskan gold) soon made that fare untenable, neither city officials nor voters were willing to grant increases. Cash-strapped and unable to modernize, streetcar companies started going under.

When they did, General Motors was waiting. In 1926, it opened a subsidiary whose job was to buy up teetering streetcar companies and replace the cars with buses. During the next thirty years, GM ripped up thousands of miles of track in New York, Los Angeles, St. Louis, Philadelphia, Baltimore, Salt Lake City—over a hundred streetcar companies in all. At length, a federal jury found General Motors guilty of criminal conspiracy. The fine was $5,000, which was less than the company made by converting a single streetcar.

General Motors was also the largest contributor to the American Road Builders Association—a lobby second in power only to the arms industry—which helped push through the Interstate Highway Act of 1956. By the authority of that act, 42,500 miles of highway were built, with the federal government picking up nine-tenths of the tab. In the postwar generation, 75 percent of government transportation spending went to highways, 1 percent to urban mass transit.

Since then, priorities have changed only slightly. In the Boston area, a working mother from Roxbury taking the subway at rush hour pays 80 percent of the cost of her trip, while a stockbroker driving his BMW back to the suburbs pays only 20 percent of the true cost of his—an arrangement that has justly been called "car welfare." Congress whets its budget ax and mutters darkly about the subsidy of almost $1 billion that goes to Amtrak: an insufferable meddling with the free market! Meanwhile, the subsidy of over $20 billion awarded the automobile —the amount spent on road construction and maintenance, traffic-law enforcement, and the like, above and beyond what is raised by gas taxes, tolls, and other user fees—is ignored.

The figure of $20 billion is very conservative, since it takes no account of costs to health, the environment, and the social fabric of the inner cities; or of the large part of the military budget that is spent to defend foreign oil. Nor does it reckon in the immense subsidies to sprawl that are hidden in credit and tax policies. Beginning in 1933, the Home Owners Loan Corporation helped to finance long-term, low-interest mortgages for home-buyers. It also invented redlining. Its appraisal system ranked neighborhoods on a color scale: green, blue, yellow, red. Newly built suburbs lived in by white professionals were green; old urban neighborhoods inhabited by blacks, Jews, or other minorities were red. Even more far-reaching in its effects was the Federal Housing Administration, set up in 1934 to insure long-term mortgages. The favorable terms it underwrote often made buying cheaper than renting. This might have been a good thing, on balance, if the FHA had not blatantly favored suburbs over cities. FHA guidelines favored free-standing single-family homes whose lot sizes, setbacks, and house widths met certain minimum standards. They favored new construction over home improvement. They even recommended restrictive covenants, so that "properties shall continue to be occupied by the same social and racial classes." With the help of the FHA, the trickle of middle-class whites leaving the cities quickly became a hemorrhage.

Many other policies, at all levels of government, have nurtured sprawl. Tax laws have favored new construction over renovation. Costs for suburban streets and sewers have often been borne by a whole city. Revenues have been siphoned off from cities and sprayed about outlying areas, notably in the form of defense spending. Low taxes on gasoline have given the driver a free ride. The mortgage-interest deduction has given rich suburbanites a subsidy several times the size of that extended to welfare families. And so on and on.

In a real sense, all of these are subsidies to the automobile. But we should not assume that they were all brought about by the car-and-oil lobby, or by any other assemblage of crude interests. For most of this century, the American public as a whole has believed that cars were the answer to many of America's problems. For the most part, its political leaders and social thinkers have thought so, too. Cars would save the cities by cleansing them of horse manure and purging them of excess population. (As Ford put it with typical bluntness: "We shall solve the city problems by leaving the city.") Cars would save the countryside by taming its great spaces and salving its loneliness. Cars would bring people back to the land.

"We can have it both ways, they say. We can enjoy our cake and at the same time destroy it, grind it to bits in the urbanizing, industrializing mill, and transform what we prize into boom time, if temporary, jobs for thousands and fat bank accounts for the tiny but powerful minority of land speculators, tract slum builders, bankers, car dealers, and shopping-mall hustlers who stand to profit from what they call growth."

—EDWARD ABBEY, *Learning to Listen to the Land*

"Like winds and sunsets, wild things were taken for granted until progress began to do away with them. Now we face the question whether a still higher 'standard of living' is worth its cost in things natural, wild and free. For us of the minority, the opportunity to see geese is more important than television, and the chance to find a pasque-flower is a right as inalienable as free speech."

—Aldo Leopold, *A Sand County Almanac*

$\rightarrow\!\!\succ\!\!\prec\!\!\leftarrow$

David Orr
Speed · 1998

Water moving too quickly through a landscape does not recharge underground aquifers. The results are floods in wet weather and droughts in the summer. Money moving too quickly through an economy does not recharge the local well-springs of prosperity, whatever else it does for that great scam called the global economy. The result is an economy polarized between those few who do well in a high-velocity economy and those left behind. Information moving too quickly to become knowledge and grow into wisdom does not recharge moral aquifers on which families, communities, and entire nations depend. The result is moral atrophy and public confusion. The common thread between all three is velocity. And they are tied together in a complex system of cause and effect that we have mostly overlooked.

There is an appropriate velocity for water set by geology, soils, vegetation, and ecological relationships in a given landscape. There is an appropriate velocity for money that corresponds to long-term needs of communities rooted in particular places and to the necessity of preserving ecological capital. There is an appropriate velocity for information, set by the assimilative capacity of the mind and by the collective learning rate of communities and entire societies. Having exceeded the speed limits, we are vulnerable to ecological degradation, economic arrangements that are unjust and unsustainable, and, in the face of great and complex problems, to befuddlement that comes with information overload.

The ecological effects of the increased velocity of water are easy to comprehend. We can see floods and, with a bit of effort, we can discern how human actions can amplify droughts. But it is harder to comprehend the social, political, economic, and ecological effects of increasing the velocity of money and information, which are often indirect and hidden. Increasing the velocity of commerce, information, and transport, however, requires more administration and regulation of human affairs to ameliorate congestion and other problems. More administration means that there are fewer productive people, higher overhead, and higher taxes to pay for more infrastructure necessitated by the speed of people and things and problems of congestion. Increasing velocity and scale tends to increase the complexity of social and ecological arrangements and reduce the time available to recognize and avoid problems. Cures for problems caused by increasing velocity often set in motion a cascading series of other problems. As a result we stumble through a succession of escalating crises with diminishing capacity to foresee and forestall. Other examples fit the same pattern, such as the velocity of transportation, material flows, extraction of nonrenewable resources, introduction of new chemicals, and human reproduction. At the local scale the effect is widening circles of disintegration and social disorder. At the global scale, the rate of change caused by increasing velocity disrupts biological evolution and the biogeochemical cycles of the Earth.

The increasing velocity of the global culture is no accident. It is the foundation of the corporate-dominated global economy that requires quick returns on investment and rapid economic growth. It is the soul of the consumer economy that feeds on impulse, obsession, and instant gratification. The velocity of water in our landscape is a direct result of too many automobiles, too much pavement, sprawling development, deforestation, and a food system that cannot be sustained in any decent or safe manner. The speed of information is driven by something that more and more resembles addiction. But above all, increasing speed is driven by minds unaware of the irony that the race has never been to the swift.

→>-<+-

GEORGE BREWSTER
Land Recycling and Sustainable Communities · *1998*

Picture a landscape that was one rugged and beautiful but is now miles upon miles of asphalt. What used to be a cornfield is now a shopping center; what used to be a two-lane country road is now a major artery through a housing subdivision. This is growth, American style—unplanned, low-density development in ever more distant suburbs, linked to the city only by new highways. Some call this progress. But for many, it evokes a sense of loss and diminution. The more our cities expand outward, the further we stray from what we really want: vibrant and livable communities, access to parks and natural areas, proximity to work, and quality time with our families and friends.

Urban sprawl has become a fact of life in nearly every corner of this nation as people move "up and out" of cities in search of a "better life" in the suburbs. A factor that has profoundly shaped the development of the nation's Western regions is the 19th-century doctrine of Manifest Destiny—the belief that the United States would inevitably expand westward to the Pacific. The rush that accompanied the opening of the West more than a century ago still feeds the deep-seated belief that land here is plentiful, cheap, and boundless. Professor Robert Burchell of the Rutgers University Center for Urban Policy and Research calls this perception that land is available in unlimited supply for development purposes the "prairie" philosophy. He notes that people feel that it is "the responsibility of both political jurisdictions and [developers] to ensure that land is ready for development, regardless of cost."

At the end of the 20th century, with the Western frontier a memory, this philosophy no longer makes sense. Yet it remains deeply rooted in the nation's psyche. As a country, we are forced to grapple with these often-unstated assumptions when making land use decisions. But can we afford to let land use and development be left to laissez-faire capitalism? Does an individual have a right to use his land for whatever he wishes, without regard for its effect on his neighbors? How wide a circle of impact should be considered? These questions frame one of the most important conflicts of our time, that of private property rights versus the individual's obligation to society as a whole, an obligation typically manifested in the form of land use regulations.

As the impact of unchecked sprawl becomes more widely recognized, this conflict grows ever more divisive and impassioned. What we are seeing around the country, and increasingly in California, is consensus among historically unaligned voices—from town planners to business interests—that something must be done to more effectively guide growth in the next century. Without thoughtful planning, maintaining a high quality of life in California will become increasingly difficult. [. . .]

Better planning for growth would also achieve benefits beyond land conservation. Putting more housing units on each acre of land decreases the land cost per housing unit, helping to provide more affordable housing. Higher concentrations of residents within walking distance of retail and entertainment businesses and public transit systems increase the viability of the businesses and the transit systems. Planned growth also increases the tax base for urban communities, boosting funding for services, schools, libraries, parks, and civic buildings.

As the 21st century is to begin, Californians have a choice: growth as a problem, or growth as part of a solution. Short-term, unplanned growth will inevitably result in a declining quality of life for all residents; sustainable growth will maintain and improve the quality of life in our cities, suburbs, and rural areas alike.

+>-<+

"We ignore the natural limit to growth at our peril. Nothing can grow forever without exhausting its resources and collapsing inward—no organism, no population, no economy. Released from their profound natural restraints, our arid-land cities have become bloated with the lifeblood of other places, vampire like. I fear for the future of these frayed hems of Denver, no longer prairie. With limits dismissed, can any sense of proper scale survive?"

—Robert Michael Pyle, *The Thunder Tree*

+>-<+

Dianne Dumanoski
Rethinking Environmentalism · 1998

These are dark times on the environmental front. What were just bad dreams in the summer of 1988 fill newspaper headlines in the summer of 1998. As anticipated, the punch of global warming is hitting faster and harder at high latitudes. Alaska is already melting. The average temperature there has jumped five degrees Fahrenheit in the past 30 years. The *New York Times,* which has been loath to alarm its readers about the global warming over the past decade, reports soberly that Alaska's glaciers are retreating rapidly, the permafrost is thawing, and the broad stretches of white spruce forest are dead and dying. Between a third and a half of the white spruce have succumbed to climate-related damage. [. . .]

Such disturbing news should bring on a new bout of despair. But I find myself feeling strangely expectant and even a bit hopeful. In my bones, I'm convinced a profound transformation is already beginning—a shift comparable in scale to the Renaissance and the Enlightenment, which remade the mental and physical worlds and launched modern civilization. Our current way of life emerged from a cultural earthquake that brought down a worldview and shattered the foundations of the existing order. Now the plates are shifting again deep beneath the surface. This is a hinge of history, a time that demands bold voices, vision, and leadership to nudge the flow of change in promising directions. Unfortunately, the American environmental community has yet to rise to the challenge of this unique historical moment. [. . .]

How, I wondered, had we arrived at this juncture? What does it say about us? Who are we anyway? Can we come to grips with our fundamentally changed situation? How do we make the dangerous passage that lies ahead? [. . .]

I fear that environmental campaigns that have captured public imagination—such as the worthy battles to save wilderness, rainforests, and dolphins—have helped foster the impression that this crisis is primarily about distant places and creatures rather than about the natural systems that support our communities and the larger human civilization. This focus on a "nature" remote from our daily lives has reinforced a dualism within our culture—which imagines a nature separate from the places where we live our lives and makes it difficult to perceive our situation clearly. President Clinton's grand symbolic gesture on the environment during his 1996 reelection campaign—his trip to Utah to announce a decision to protect the Grand Staircase–Escalante National Monument—speaks volumes in this regard. If this is what his political advisors think will play with voters and the environmental community, it is a troubling sign indeed. The nature that we need to save is not a place and the highest stakes, in my opinion, are not endangered species or stunning pieces of red rock desert, though these are precious indeed. This double vision supports the comforting delusion that we can somehow save half the world while the degradation accelerates elsewhere and it obscures the reality that the human civilization we pass on to our children and grandchildren is also in profound jeopardy. [. . .]

As I see it, the new wave of American environmental activism born in the late 1960s has been floundering about for the past three decades in part because it is mired in an unresolved philosophical crisis and a stalled transition. This crisis, which surfaced in the shadow of the bomb and the chemical revolution after World War II, arose because it became increasingly difficult to sustain the dualism—which divides the world into sacred nature and profane lands of human habitation—that has long been a part of the Romantic tradition and environmental thought. To understand this double vision, one needs to know a little bit about its origins. Most contemporary environmental battles reflect an ongoing feud within western civilization that has been raging for more than three centuries over the uses of nature and the human place in the larger scheme of things. [. . .]

Could there be nature on a human-dominated planet? Not the nature of the Romantic tradition or of Carson's nature writing, it seems. If this is the case, then the environmental tradition needs some major philosophical reconstruction. It needs to put hard work into laying a new foundation that will bear the weight of a changed world and carry it confidently forward to meet this altered reality. Though there has been much philosophical debate over such issues as "anthropocentrism" versus "biocentrism," I don't think it has moved us in the right direction, for the argument wallows in the dualism that has been obsolete for half a century now. [. . .]

Given the record, one has to question the wisdom of this crisis-oriented activism. Is there any value in running faster and faster to keep up with the accelerating treadmill of crisis? Perhaps the time has come to forget the brush fires and take on the pyromaniac.

I don't have a glib prescription to offer, but I am certain that those who care about the environment and the future need to confront these unresolved issues head on. Some of my own conclusions are already evident. If this modern global civilization survives the next few centuries, it will only do so through a profound transformation that will alter all of its current operating assumptions. While some within the environmental community have turned their attention to fundamental flaws in the system and the need to alter assumptions, far too much energy has gone into battling for mitigation of symptoms. [. . .]

I have old and dear friends, who have spent their lives trying to stop the hemorrhaging of natural systems and the devastation of beautiful places. They take serious issue with my conclusions, arguing that these efforts have to continue. Otherwise, they contend, we will have nothing left by the time the new order emerges. I respect these efforts deeply but I question whether this strategy will save anything at all. To me, it has become increasingly clear that the only long-term hope for the places and things that have inspired the environmental imagination is a speedy move toward the new order. Species are disappearing even in protected areas like Yosemite National Park, where five of seven species of frogs and toads have vanished in the past century without explanation. These losses, which may be due to pesticide contamination traveling into the Sierra from California agricultural areas, bear witness to our failed experiment with double vision. In the face of rising sea levels, one of my friends is trying to buy and preserve an exquisite, low-lying coral atoll in the Pacific. I see this as an environmental parable for our times.

So let's assume that the environmental community heeds this counsel. What are the ingredients of an environmental effort equal to the times? Boldness and vision stand at the top of the list. If those concerned about the environment want to move global civilization in a new direction, they first need to get to work on developing a broad, compelling, and coherent vision that will provide a map for the human future. To rank as a serious contender, such a vision must reach beyond the traditional boundaries of environmental thought and describe how leading institutions in our global civilization—such as science, technology, and the economy—need to be redirected in light of our changed situation. This vision needs to unmask the deepest assumptions of the current order, many of them rather recent philosophical inventions as it turns out. This means taking on the guiding myths of modern life—notions that are so much a part of the current worldview that many people take them to be truths rather than assumptions. It should be noted, however, that the environmental tradition springs from the same 18th-century soil as the rest of modern culture and it shares some of its problematic assumptions, including the fiction of individualism that emerged in this period.

Any serious challenge to our current civilization also needs to address the deepest philosophical questions. At this critical moment in the human journey, we must grapple with the question of human purpose in the light of our altered circumstance and of how we ought to live. We need to consider how we bring liberty and limits into reasonable balance. We need to confront the question that haunts modern life and seems to ring with increasing hollowness: freedom for what? Surely these times demand a more imaginative answer than "the pursuit of happiness."

My own list of obsolete and increasingly dangerous concepts in need of revision includes: current notions of individualism, private property, and unmanaged markets and global free trade.

Chapter 3: The Boundaries Between Us

This chapter asks us to reconsider all of the boundaries in our lives, and, in so doing, makes more clear the social and legal obstacles to a land ethic. Boundaries can divide people from places and also people from one another. While land conservation is ultimately about reducing physical boundaries, by changing private land into public land, it can also begin to diminish social and cultural boundaries. At its best, land conservation leads to social change by tearing down the walls that divide people from themselves, from each other, and from nature, and thus becomes the starting point for a renewed civic life. Land conservation gives a person something—a place, an idea, a belief, a relationship—to share with someone they don't know, or may otherwise never be able to know, thereby creating a bond. It is here that land conservation begins to move us from isolation to community.

Is it possible to create a land ethic in a society so devoted at so many levels to "good fences?" How might we help each other to find nature, find our own human community, and redefine how we live on the land?

→>−<+−

"The first man who, having fenced in a piece of land, said, 'This is mine' and found people naive enough to believe him, that man was the true founder of a civil society."

—JEAN JACQUES ROUSSEAU

→>−<+−

The earth was formed whole and continuous in the universe, without lines.

The human mind arose in the universe needing lines, boundaries, distinctions. Here and not there. This and not that. Mine and not yours.

That is sea and this is land, and here is the line between them. See? It's very clear on the map.

But, as the linguists say, the map is not the territory. The line on the map is not to be found at the edge of the sea.

Humans build houses on the land beside the sea, and the sea comes and takes them away.

That is not land, says the sea. It is also not sea. Look at the territory, which God created, not the map, which you created. There is no place where land ends and sea begins.

The places that are not-land, not-sea, are beautiful, functional, fecund. Humans do not treasure them. In fact, they barely see them because those spaces do not fit the lines in the mind. Humans keep busy dredging, filling, building, diking, draining the places between land and sea, trying to make them either one or the other.

Here is the line, the mind says, between Poland and Russia, between France and Germany, between Jordan and Israel. Here is the Iron Curtain between East and West. Here is the line around the United States, separating us from not-us. It's very clear here, on the map.

The cosmonauts and astronauts in space (cosmonauts are theirs, astronauts are ours) look down and see no lines. They are created only by minds. They shift in history as minds change.

On the earth's time-scale, human-invented lines shift very quickly. The maps of fifty years ago, of 100 years ago, of 1,000 years ago are very different from the maps of today. The planet is 4 billion years old. Human lines are ephemeral, though people kill one another over them.

Even during the fleeting moments of planetary time when the lines between nations are held still, immigrants cross them legally and illegally. Money and goods cross them legally and illegally. Migrating birds cross them, acid rain crosses them, radioactive debris from Chernobyl crosses them. Ideas cross them with the speed of sound and light. Even where Idea Police stand guard, ideas are not stopped by lines. How could they be? The lines are themselves only ideas.

Between me and not-me there is surely a line, a clear distinction, or so it seems. But now that I look, where is that line?

This fresh apple, still cold and crisp from the morning dew, is not-me only until I eat it. When I eat, I eat the soil that nourished the apple. When I drink, the waters of the earth become me. With every breath I take in I draw in not-me and make it me. With every breath out, I exhale me into not-me.

If the air and the waters and the soils are poisoned, I am poisoned. Only if I believe the fiction of the lines more than the truth of the lineless planet will I poison the earth, which is myself.

Between you and me, now there is certainly a line. No other line feels more certain than that one. Sometimes it seems not a line but a canyon, a yawning empty space across which I cannot reach.

Yet you keep appearing in my awareness. Even when you are far away, something of you surfaces constantly in my wandering thoughts. When you are nearby, I feel your presence, I sense your mood. Even when I try not to. Especially when I try not to.

If you are on the other side of the planet, if I don't know your name, if you speak a language I don't understand, even then, when I see a picture of your face, full of joy, I feel your joy. When your face shows suffering, I feel that too. Even when I try not to. Especially then.

I have to work hard not to pay attention to you. When I succeed, when I close my mind to you with walls of indifference, then the presence of those walls, which constrain my own aliveness, are reminders of the you to whom I would rather not pay attention.

When I do pay attention, very close attention, when I open myself fully to your humanity, your complexity, your reality, then I find, always, under every other feeling and judgment and emotion, that I love you.

Even between you and me, even there, the lines are only of our own making.

→>-<←

"Bought nothing. Because He told in the Book how He created the earth, made it and looked at it and said it was all right, and then He made man. He made the earth first and peopled it with dumb creatures, and then He created man to be His overseer on the earth and to hold suzerainty over the earth and the animals on it in His name, not to hold for himself and his descendants inviolable title forever, generation after generation to the oblongs and squares of the earth, but to hold the earth mutual and intact in the communal anonymity of brotherhood and all the fee He asked was pity and humility and sufferance and endurance and the sweat of his face for bread."

—WILLIAM FAULKNER, *The Bear*

→►◄←

GERALD HAUSMAN
Turtle Island Alphabet · *1991*

A mother, by definition, is one who gives birth to and cares for her children. Thus, the Indian concept of the nurturing source of all good comes from within, not from without, the fecundity of maternal earth. This is a spiritual rather than a material relationship to land. The idea is far removed from the white European notion of land being something to give tenure to, something to own, something from which to reap benefit.

Furthermore, the Native American Earth Mother value system was a great deal more than that: It was religion. Property and self-aggrandizement, that which arises from ownership of land, was a desecration of Indian religion. You do not take from the Mother; she gives freely to those whose reverence is declared by familial responsibility; sonhood and daughterhood are rewarded with nourishment and love. (The same familial, tribal union exists in the Hebrew translation of the Old Testament of the Bible. Yahweh rewards those to whom the sacrifice of love and obedience is innate and unpremeditated. In this sense, even though Yahweh is a symbol of fatherhood, he shows a dual nature, a mothering tendency, and acts as both mother and father to his children.)

Mother, being impartial, could not offer her blessing to one of her children and not to another (this differs in large measure with the Old Testament Yahweh). Therefore, the Native American Earth Mother would not allow her flesh, the land itself, to be appropriated by one individual or tribe, to the exclusion of any other(s). All must benefit—or none. This was the way it was, and still is.

This idea of impartial motherhood was once explained to me by a Navajo friend, Ray Brown, who said that though the Sun Father was a powerful deity, his very power and strength could overwhelm (Yahweh destroying the cities of Sodom and Gomorrah) Earth Surface People. Yet not so with Mother Earth. The Sun Father might burn a man with all-powerful rays, and Changing Woman, the Earth Mother, with the proper herbs, would heal the burn and make it well again. Always, the Mother restrains and protects her offspring, birthing and helping and healing.

The attitude of sharing the goodness of Mother Earth is opposed to the selfish individuation of land tenure, which may be defined as a secular tending of the earth. Instead of depending on the outflow of mother's milk, so to speak, man, uncertain of mother's love, takes control of the soil and works it his way.

In doing so, he becomes an occupant of the area he tends and the place from which he derives food is his dependency, his place of tenure. Although the Pueblo Indians of the Southwest, in particular, "tended" the land, they also worshiped it. [. . .]

Frank Hamilton Cushing, the great observer of the Zuni people, said that a Zuni man might farm a field of unclaimed land, and it would then belong to him. However, in truth, it was considered the property of his clan. Upon his death, the land might be cultivated by any member of his clan (but not by his wife or children, who must be of another clan). Indians of other tribes in North America often fought among themselves over desirable territory, such as hunting and fishing grounds. While dealing in occupancy, however, they did not consider land as merchantable; instead it was seen as life-sustainable.

In recent times, the conflict of land as merchandise and land as mother came up in the 1930s. John Steinbeck's *The Grapes of Wrath* is a biblical treatise of white society in modern America: land ownership versus land nurtureship. When Rose of Sharon offers her breast to the old man and saves his life with her mother's milk, the point is clearly made. Those who care for the earth also care for one another. The sharing is unilateral. This is a clear and definite Native American, earth-worship, tribal value system.

In 1783, the Continental Congress forbade private purchase or acceptance of lands from Indians. On the adoption of the Constitution, the right of eminent domain became vested in the United States, and Congress alone had the power to extinguish the Indians' right of occupancy.

In 1887, 104 years later, the Dawes Act provided that every

Native American was to be given "a piece of reservation." The surplus land, that which was left over, was purchasable by the United States government for $1.25 per acre. In 1933, forty-six years later, Indian-owned land had dwindled from 138 million to 52 million acres.

In 1865, the Duwamish chief Seattle, speaking of land ownership, said something that has often been quoted. It seems to contain the very atom of disagreement between the two anatomically different cultures, Indian and white:

> How can you buy or sell the sky—the warmth of the land? The idea is strange to us. We do not own the freshness of the air or the sparkle of the water. How can you buy them from us? . . . We know that the white man does not understand our way. One portion of the land is the same to him as the next, for he is a stranger who comes in the night and takes from the land whatever he needs. . . .

→>-<+

JAMES HOWARD KUNSTLER
The Geography of Nowhere · *1993*

American land law was predicated on the paramount principle that land was first and foremost a commodity for capital gain. Speculation became the primary basis for land distribution—indeed, the commercial transfer of property would become the basis of American land-use planning, which is to say hardly any planning at all. Somebody would buy a large tract of land and subdivide it into smaller parcels at a profit—a process that continues in our time.

Other Old World values toppled before this novel system—for example, the idea of land as the physical container for community values. Nearly eradicated in the rush to profit was the concept of stewardship, of land as a public trust: that we who are alive now are responsible for taking proper care of the landscape so that future generations can dwell in it in safety and happiness. As historian Sam Bass Warner put it, the genius of American land law and the fanatical support it engendered "lay in its identification of land as a civil liberty instead of as a social resource."

This is embodied today in the popular phrase, "You can't tell me what to do with my land." The "you" here might be a neighbor, the community, or the government. The government's power to regulate land use was limited under the Fifth and Fourteenth Amendments to the Constitution. The Fifth states that private property cannot be taken for public use without due process of law and just compensation—the right to public hearings and payment at market value—and the Fourteenth reiterates the due process clause. All subsequent land-use law in America has hinged on whether it might deprive somebody of the economic value of their land.

America's were the most liberal property laws on earth when they were established. The chief benefits were rapid development of the wilderness, equal opportunity for those with cash and/or ambition, simplicity of acquisition, and the right to exploitation—such as chopping down all the virgin white pine forests of Michigan (they called it "mining trees"). Our laws gave the individual clear title to make his own decisions, but they also deprived him of the support of community and custom and of the presence of sacred places.

The identification of this extreme individualism of property ownership with all that is sacred in American life has been the source of many of the problems. . . . Above all, it tends to degrade the idea of the public realm, and hence of the landscape tissue that ties together the thousands of pieces of private property that make up a town, a suburb, a state. It also degrades the notion that the private individual has a responsibility to his public realm—or, to put it another way, that the public realm is the physical manifestation of the common good.

Tocqueville observed this when he toured America in 1831. "Individualism," he wrote, "at first, only saps the virtues of public life; but in the long run it attacks and destroys all others and is at length absorbed in selfishness."

→>-<←

WENDELL BERRY
Another Turn of the Crank · 1995

In my own politics and economics I am a Jeffersonian—or, I might more accurately say, I am a democrat and an agrarian. I believe that land that is to be used should be divided into small parcels among a lot of small owners; I believe therefore in the right of private property. I believe that, given our history and tradition, a large population of small property holders offers the best available chance for local cultural adaptation and good stewardship of the land—provided that the property holders are secure, legally and economically, in their properties.

To say that the right of private property has often been used to protect individuals and even global corporations in their greed is not to say that it cannot secure individuals in an appropriate economic share in their country and in a consequent economic and political independence, just as Thomas Jefferson thought it could. That is the political justification of the right of private property. There is also, I believe, an ecological justification. If landed properties are democratically divided and properly scaled, and if family security in these properties can be preserved over a number of generations, then we will greatly increase the possibility of authentic cultural adaptation to local homelands. Not only will we make more apparent to successive generations the necessary identity between the health of human communities and the health of local ecosystems but we will also give people the best motives for caretaking and we will call into service the necessary local intelligence and imagination. Such an arrangement would give us the fullest possible assurance that our forests and farmlands would be used by people who know them best and care the most about them.

My interest here is in preserving the possibility of intimacy in the use of the land. Some of us still understand the elaborate care necessary to preserve marital and familial and social intimacy, but I am arguing also for the necessity of preserving silvicultural and agricultural intimacy. The possibility of intimacy between worker and place is virtually identical with the possibility of good work. True intimacy in work, as in love, means lifelong commitment; it means knowing what you are doing. The industrial consumer and the industrial producer believe that after any encounter between people or between people and the world there will be no consequences. The consumptive society is interested in sterile or inconsequential intimacy, which is a fantasy. But suppose, on the contrary, that we try to serve the cultural forms and imperatives that prepare adequately for the convergence of need with fertility, of human life with the natural world. *Then* we must think of consequences; we must think of the children.

I am an uneasy believer in the right of private property because I know that this right can be understood as the right to destroy property, which is to say the natural or the given world. I do not believe that such a right exists, even though its presumed existence has covered the destruction of a lot of land. A considerable amount of this destruction has been allowed by our granting to corporations the status of "persons" capable of holding "private property." Most corporate abuse or destruction of land must be classified, I think, as either willing or intentional. The willingness to use land on a large scale implies inevitably at least a willingness to damage it. But because we have had, alongside our history of land abuse, a tradition or at least a persistent hope of agrarian economy and settled community life, the damage to the land that has been done by individual owners is more likely to be attributable to ignorance or to economic constraint. To speak sensibly of property and of the rights and uses of property, we must always observe this fundamental distinction between corporate property and prosperity that is truly private—that is, property of modest or appropriate size owned by an individual.

--><--

"Walls, no less than writing, define civilization. They are monuments of resistance against time, like writing itself. Walls protect, divide, distinguish; above all they abstract. Gilgamesh is the builder of such walls that divide history from prehistory, culture from nature, sky from earth, life from death, memory from oblivion."

—ROBERT POGUE HARRISON, *Forest: A Shadow of Civilization*

WILLIAM CRONON
Changes in the Land · *1983*

In the long run, it was [the] conception of land as private commodity rather than public commons that came to typify New England towns. Initial divisions of town lands, with their functional classifications of woodlot and meadow and cornfield, bore a superficial resemblance to Indian usufruct rights, since they seemed to define land in terms of how it was to be used. Once transferred into private hands, however, most such lands became abstract parcels whose legal definition bore no inherent relation to their use: a person owned everything on them, not just specific activities which could be conducted within their boundaries. Whereas the earliest deeds tended to describe land in terms of its topography and use—for instance, as the mowing field between a certain two creeks—later deeds described land in terms of lots held by adjacent owners, and marked territories using the surveyor's abstractions of points of the compass and metes and bounds. Recording systems, astonishingly sloppy in the beginning because there was little

English precedent for them, became increasingly formalized so that boundaries could be more precisely defined. Even Indian deeds showed this transformation. The land Pynchon purchased from the Agawam village was vaguely defined in terms of cornfields, meadows, and the Connecticut River; an eighteenth-century deed from the same county, on the other hand, transferred rights to two entire townships which it defined precisely but abstractly as "the full Contents of Six miles in Weadth and Seven miles in length," starting from a specified point.

The uses to which land could be put vanished from such descriptions, and later land divisions increasingly ignored actual topography. What was on the land became largely irrelevant to its legal identity, even though its contents—and the rights them —might still have great bearing on the price it would bring if sold. Describing land as a fixed parcel with purely arbitrary boundaries made buying and selling it increasingly easy, as did the recording systems—an American innovation—which kept track of such transactions. Indeed, legal descriptions, however abstracted, had little effect on everyday life *until* land was sold. People did not cease to be intimately a part of the land's ecology simply by reason of the language with which their deeds were written. But when it came time to transfer property rights, those deeds allowed the alienation of land as a commodity, an action with important ecological consequences. To the abstraction of legal boundaries was added the abstraction of price, a measurement of property's value assessed on a unitary scale. More than anything else, it was the treatment of land and property as commodities traded at market that distinguished English conceptions of ownership from Indian ones. [. . .]

The difference between Indians and Europeans was not that one had property and the other had none; rather, it was that they loved property differently. Timothy Dwight, writing at the beginning of the nineteenth century, lamented the fact that Indians had not yet learned the love of property. "Wherever this can be established," he said, "Indians may be civilized; wherever it cannot, they will still remain Indians." The statement was truer than he probably realized. Speaking strictly in terms of precolonial New England, Indian conceptions of property were central to Indian uses of the land, and Indians could not live as Indians had lived unless the land was owned as Indians had owned it. Conversely, the land could not long remain unchanged if it were owned in a different way. The sweeping alterations of the colonial landscape which Dwight himself so shrewdly described were testimony that a people who loved property little had been overwhelmed by a people who loved it much.

→>◄‹

ERIC FREYFOGLE
Bounded People, Boundless Lands · *1998*

Like many of Robert Frost's poems, "Mending Wall" is a study in contradiction. Set in rural New England, it is a narrative poem about boundaries and walls, in nature, culture, and the human mind. As the poem opens, spring has arrived in rocky farm country, and with it has come an annual ritual: the mending of the stone wall that divides the narrator's farm from his neighbor's. Choosing a date as they have done before, the two farmers walk their shared wall together, each replacing the stones on his side. While the work proceeds, the narrator muses about the rocky wall, his stern-faced neighbor, and the jumbled ways in which people and land fit together. From the neighbor comes only a single sentence. Twice repeated, it is the line of the poem that has become best known: "Good fences make good neighbors."

American culture has latched on to this proverb, no doubt because it captures so well a number of tendencies and assumptions that seem so sensible. We like fences and erect them often, routinely separating "mine" from "yours." We like to divide land and instinctively think of land as parceled and bounded. Frost, however, didn't mean to endorse this adage outright, and the narrator in "Mending Wall" is intent on challenging it. "Something there is," the narrator says, "that doesn't love a wall, / That wants it down." The frozen-ground-swell" of winter "spills the upper boulders in the sun; / And makes gaps even two can pass abreast." Nature, it seems, dislikes this stone wall. Freezing and thawing work against it, and so does gravity. Wandering hunters also play a role, knocking down stones to "have the rabbit out of hiding." Then there are the more mysterious forces that seem secretly to pull at stone walls. Elves at work, the narrator speculates, "but it's not elves exactly." However caused, the wall's gaps appear yearly: "No one has seen them made or heard them made, / But at spring mending-time we find them there."

"Something there is that doesn't love a wall, / That wants it down."

"Good fences make good neighbors."

As Frost's narrator relates his tale of labor shared, he argues for his side of this enduring tension. The stone wall has no purpose, he points out. The neighbor's farm "is all pine and I am apple orchard. / My apple trees will never get across / And eat the cones under his pines. . . ." Walls make sense when there are cows, "but here there are no cows." So why do fences make good neighbors? the narrator demands to know— silently asking of himself and of the reader but not, importantly, of his neighbor. "Before I built a wall I'd ask to know / What I was walling in or walling out, / And to whom I was like to give offence."

Throughout the poem, Frost seems tilted toward the narrator's view of things, but the poem takes a turn at the end. It is the tradition-tied neighbor who has the last say. "Good fences make good neighbors," he says again, proud that he has thought of the idea. There the poem ends, and the mending work goes on.

"Mending Wall," one of Frost's classics, raises enduring questions about owning and living on the land. Why are fences and boundaries so attractive, Frost implicitly asks, when nature itself is boundless? How do they reflect the perceptions and values of a particular culture? How have people used them, for good and ill, to shape the land as well as their own lives? "A good poem," American novelist and poet Robert Penn Warren once noted, "drops a stone into the pool of our being, and the ripples spread." In the case of "Mending Wall" the ripples set loose are many, and they spread in various ways—outward across the land, backward into history, and inward, into the reaches of human nature.

Frost is clear on only one point: nature has no need for walls, stone or otherwise. When it comes to human needs, his narrative is less definitive. Cows have a habit of wandering, which means that for cattle owners, at least, walls are a positive good. For hunters, walls are a nuisance, if not a danger; game animals don't respect them, so hunters won't either. Orchard owners, needing no walls, think of their maintenance as mostly aimless work—though Frost's narrator is able to view his labor lightly, as "just another kind of out-door game."

With these points made, Frost has covered the practical aspects of walls: They are useful for some purposes, bothersome for others. As readers we're left to consider why people like walls so much and how walls reflect and shape who people are. Why do good fences make good neighbors? Is there something inherently appealing about boundaries? Is there something in a person's ability to witness the land, to grasp it in the mind, to sink roots into it and take responsibility for it, that somehow generates the drive to divide? Nature may need no sharp boundaries, but do people?

In the "good fences" adage, nature is a storehouse of commodities, a collection of discrete parts, not an intermingled whole. An alternative view, expressed by the poem's narrator, displays a willingness to set aside tradition and listen to nature, particularly nature's messages about connectedness and interdependence. As the questioning narrator sees it, his neighbor's yearning for boundaries reflects a territorial longing that reaches back to the Stone Age. Indeed, so culturally entrenched is this longing that in the end the narrator bows to it, never mustering the courage to voice his doubts.

Implicit in Frost's poem, unmentioned by either farmer, is a third aspect of this stone wall—its symbolism of communal cooperation, of neighbors identifying a shared goal and working together to achieve it. This tradition thrives in the springtime ritual of mending, which carries on year after year. Frost never explains why his narrator ultimately holds his tongue, but the farmer's reticence probably has more to do with the maintenance of communal bonds than with any pleasure he derives from his "outdoor game." By respecting the wall-mending tradition, the narrator admits that he and his neighbor benefit from a peaceful coexistence. Good neighbors get along, and in getting along they foster the well-being of the whole. [. . .]

American and other Western cultures have been overly inclined to divide the natural world into pieces and to see the land community not as a blurred mosaic of ecosystems but as a collection of homesteads, water flows, and natural resources. The same tendency toward division and separation shows up in the social realm, where human society is understood as a collection of individuals. But the more a society emphasizes boundaries—the more weight it gives to property lines and individual autonomy—the more it denigrates the natural and social fabrics. Boundaries have their uses, but once they are constructed and respected, they take on lives of their own, constricting the vision, understanding, and behavior of the people who've erected them. In all likelihood, the neighbor in Robert Frost's "Mending Wall" understood the land and his place on it far differently because of the stone wall and what the wall meant to him and his home culture.

On the eve of the new century, Americans are much in need of a more poetic sense of the land, a sense of its organic wholeness and beauty; its inner motion and energy, its subtle music and spirituality. To tend the land wisely is not just to use it efficiently; it is to recognize the land's sacredness and show it due respect.

→>-<←

"The significance of space in landscape terms . . . is that it makes the social order visible. The network of boundaries, private as well as public, transforms an amorphous environment into a human landscape, and nothing more clearly shows some of the cherished values of a group than the manner in which they fix those boundaries, the manner in which they organize space."

—J. B. Jackson, *Discovering the Vernacular Landscape*

→>-<←

N. Scott Momaday
The Man Made of Words · *1997*

Once in his life a man ought to concentrate his mind upon the remembered earth, I believe. He ought to give himself up to a particular landscape in his experience, to look at it from as many angles as he can, to wonder about it, to dwell upon it. He ought to imagine that he touches it with his hands at every season and listens to the sounds that are made upon it. He ought to imagine the creatures there and all the faintest motions of the wind. He ought to recollect the glare of noon and all the colors of the dawn and dusk. [. . .]

I am interested in the way that a man looks at a given landscape and takes possession of it in his blood and brain. For this happens, I am certain, in the ordinary motion of life. None of us lives apart from the land entirely; such an isolation is unimaginable. We have sooner or later to come to terms with the world around us—and I mean especially the physical world, not only as it is revealed to us immediately through our senses, but also as it is perceived more truly in the long turn of seasons and of years. And we must come to moral terms. There is no alternative, I believe, if we are to realize and maintain our humanity, for our humanity must consist in part in the ethical as well as in the practical ideal of preservation. And particularly here and now is that true. We Americans need now more than ever before—and indeed more than we know—to imagine who and what we are with respect to the earth and sky. I am talking about an act of the imagination, essentially, and the concept of an American land ethic.

It is no doubt more difficult to imagine the landscape of America now, than it was in, say, 1900. Our whole experience as a nation in this century has been a repudiation of the pastoral ideal which informs so much of the art and literature of the nineteenth century. One effect of the technological revolution has been to uproot us from the soil. We have become disoriented, I believe; we have suffered a kind of psychic dislocation of ourselves in time and space. We may be perfectly sure of where we are in relation to the supermarket and the next coffee break, but I doubt that any of us knows where he is in relation to the stars and to the solstices. Our sense of the natural order has become dull and unreliable. Like the wilderness itself, our sphere of instinct has diminished in proportion as we have failed to imagine truly what it is. And yet I believe that it is possible to formulate an ethical idea of the land—a notion of what it is and must be in our daily lives—and I believe moreover that it is absolutely necessary to do so.

It would seem on the surface of things that a land ethic is something that is alien to, or at least dormant in, most Americans. Most of us have developed an attitude of indifference toward the land. In terms of my own experience, it is difficult to see how such an attitude could ever have come about.

II : THE POLES OF THE MOVEMENT

"In wildness is the preservation of the world."

—HENRY DAVID THOREAU

"In human culture is the preservation of wildness."

—WENDELL BERRY

→>-<-

The next two chapters present an evolution of thinking that has brought us from wilderness to ecology, from John Muir to Wendell Berry, from protecting distant wild lands to honoring the wild at home. The crucial question in this long and important story is how land conservation can evolve from providing ethics for some to ethics for all.

The wilderness movement, starting with John Muir, taught us to preserve great monuments to wildness as icons of place, and that led us, over time and after much effort, to believe that the wild was something that could only be found in wilderness. The 100-year shift in our movement toward the values of ecology and stewardship has defined the wild as a quality of being, something that is available anywhere, while wilderness is a specific place. Protecting the wild in nature and in our human hearts is the ultimate point of land conservation, but here we ask, is it the idea or the place that matters most?

When we focus primarily on preserving the place, the lessons and ethics found by being in that wilderness are available largely to those whose education and means enable the fulfillment of a wanderlust. In focusing on preserving the idea of the wild, we are more able to bring conservation home directly into our everyday lives, to replace wanderlust with homesickness. We see in the readings in these two chapters how a value or attitude of "how we are in the world" is also a fundamentally important lesson from nature and the wild and one that can be taught to anyone because it is everywhere.

Chapter 4: A Wild Idea

"Man always kills the things he loves, and so we the pioneers have killed our wilderness. Some say we had to. Be that as it may, I am glad that I shall never be young without wild country to be young in. Of what avail are forty freedoms without a blank spot on the map?"

—ALDO LEOPOLD, *A Sand County Almanac*

WALLACE STEGNER
The Wilderness Letter · 1960

I want to speak for the wilderness idea as something that has helped form our character and that has certainly shaped our history as a people. It has no more to do with recreation than churches have to do with recreation, or than the strenuousness and optimism and expansiveness of what historians call the "American Dream" have to do with recreation. Nevertheless, since it is only in this recreation survey that the values of wilderness are being compiled, I hope you will permit me to insert this idea between the leaves, as it were, of the recreation report.

Something will have gone out of us as a people if we ever let the remaining wilderness be destroyed; if we permit the last virgin forests to be turned into comic books and plastic cigarette cases; if we drive the few remaining members of the wild species into zoos or to extinction; if we pollute the last clear air and dirty the last clean streams and push our paved roads through the last of the silence, so that never again will Americans be free in their own country from the noise, the exhausts, the stinks of human and automotive waste. And so that never again can we have the chance to see ourselves single, separate, vertical, and individual in the world, part of the environment of trees and rocks and soil, brother to the other animals, part of the natural world and competent to belong in it. Without any remaining wilderness we are committed wholly, without chance for even momentary reflection and rest, to a headlong drive into our technological termite-life, the Brave New World of a completely man-controlled environment. We need wilderness preserved—as much of it as is still left, and as many kinds—because it was the challenge against which our character as a people was formed. The reminder and the reassurance that it is still there is good for our spiritual health even if we never once in ten years set foot in it. It is good for us when we are young, because of the incomparable sanity it can bring briefly, as vacation and rest, into our insane lives. It is important to us when we are old simply because it is there—important, that is, simply as idea.

We are a wild species, as Darwin pointed out. Nobody ever tamed or domesticated or scientifically bred us. But for at least three millennia we have been engaged in a cumulative and ambitious race to modify and gain control of our environment, and in the process we have come close to domesticating ourselves. Not many people are likely, any more, to look upon what we call "progress" as an unmixed blessing. Just as surely as it has brought us increased comfort and more material goods, it has brought us spiritual losses, and it threatens now to become the Frankenstein that will destroy us. One means of sanity is to retain a hold on the natural world, to remain, insofar as we can, good animals. Americans still have that chance, more than many peoples; for while we were demonstrating ourselves the most efficient and ruthless environment-busters in history, and slashing and burning and cutting our way through a wilderness continent, the wilderness was working on us. It remains in us as surely as Indian names remain on the land. If the abstract dream of human liberty and human dignity became, in America, something more than an abstract dream, mark it down at least partially to the fact that we were in subtle ways subdued by what we conquered. [. . .]

It seems to me significant that the distinct downturn in our literature from hope to bitterness took place almost at the precise time when the frontier officially came to an end, in 1890, and when the American way of life had begun to turn strongly urban and industrial. The more urban it has become, and the more frantic with technological change, the sicker and more embittered our literature, and I believe our people, have become. For myself, I grew up on the empty plains of Saskatchewan and Montana and in the mountains of Utah, and I put a very high valuation on what those places gave me. And if

I had not been able periodically to renew myself in the mountains and deserts of western America I would be very nearly bughouse. Even when I can't get to the back country, the thought of the colored deserts of southern Utah, or the reassurance that there are still stretches of prairie where the world can be instantaneously perceived as disk and bowl, and where the little but intensely important human being is exposed to the five directions and the thirty-six winds, is a positive consolation. The idea alone can sustain me. But as the wilderness areas are progressively exploited or "improved," as the jeeps and bulldozers of uranium prospectors scar up the deserts and the roads are cut into the alpine timberlands, and as the remnants of the unspoiled and natural world are progressively eroded, every such loss is a little death in me. In us. [. . .]

These are some of the things wilderness can do for us. That is the reason we need to put into effect, for its preservation, some other principle than the principles of exploitation or "usefulness" or even recreation. We simply need that wild country available to us, even if we never do more than drive to its edge and look in. For it can be a means of reassuring ourselves of our sanity as creatures, a part of the geography of hope.

"Relegating grizzlies to Alaska is about like relegating happiness to heaven; one may never get there."

—ALDO LEOPOLD, *A Sand County Almanac*

TERRY TEMPEST WILLIAMS
Testimony · *1995*

What do we wish for?

To be whole. To be complete. Wildness reminds us what it means to be human, what we are connected to rather than what we are separate from. "Our troubles," Pulitzer-prize winning scientist Edward O. Wilson writes, "arise from the fact that we do not know what we are and cannot agree on what we want to be. . . . Humanity is part of nature, a species that evolved among other species. The more closely we identify ourselves with the rest of life, the more quickly we will be able to discover the sources of human sensibility and acquire knowledge on which an enduring ethic, a sense of preferred direction, can be built."

Wilderness is both the bedrock of lands of southern Utah and a metaphor of "unlimited possibility." The question must be asked, "How can we cut ourselves off from the very source of our creation?"

This is not about economics. This is not about the preservation of ranching culture in America. And it is especially not about settling a political feud once and for all. This is about putting ourselves in accordance with nature, of consecrating these lands by remembering our relationships to them. A strong wilderness bill as recommended by Congressman Maurice Hinchey, HR 1500, is an act of such consecration. At a recent family gathering, my uncle Richard Tempest, a former Republican state senator, said simply, "Wilderness is a feeling."

Mr. Chairman, if you knew wilderness in the way that you

know love, you would be unwilling to let it go. We are talking about the body of the beloved, not real estate. We must ask ourselves as Americans, "Can we really survive the worship of our own destructiveness?" We do not exist in isolation. Our sense of community and compassionate intelligence must be extended to all life forms, plants, animals, rocks, rivers, and human beings. This is the story of our past and it will be the story of our future.

Senate Bill 884 falls desperately short of these ideals.

Who can say how much of nature can be destroyed without consequence? Who can say how much land can be used for extractive purposes until it is rendered barren forever? And who can say what the human spirit will be crying out for one hundred years from now? Two hundred years from now? A few weeks ago, Yosemite National Park had to close their gates and not allow any more visitors entry. The park was overcrowded. Last week, Yellowstone reported traffic gridlocks in the Lamar Valley, carloads of families with the wish of seeing a wolf. Did our country's lawmakers who held the vision of national parks in the nineteenth century dream of this kind of hunger? In the same vein, can you as our lawmakers today toward the end of the twentieth century imagine what the sanctity of wilderness in Utah might hold for us as a people at the turn of the twenty-first century?

We must act with this kind of vision and concern not just for ourselves, but for our children and our children's children. This is our natural heritage. And we are desperate for visionary leadership.

It's strange how deserts turn us into believers. I believe in walking in a landscape of mirages, because you learn humility. I believe in living in a land of little water, because life is drawn together. And I believe in the gathering of bones as a testament to spirits that have moved on.

If the desert is holy, it is because it is a forgotten place that allows us to remember the sacred. Perhaps that is why every pilgrimage to the desert is a pilgrimage to the self. There is no place to hide and so we are found.

Wilderness courts our souls. When I sat in church throughout my growing years, I listened to teachings about Christ walking in the wilderness for forty days and forty nights, reclaiming his strength, where he was able to say to Satan, "Get thee hence." And when I imagined Joseph Smith kneeling in a grove of trees as he received his vision to create a new religion, I believed their sojourns into nature were sacred. Are ours any less?

"To stand at the edge of the sea, to sense the ebb and the flow of the tides, to feel the breath of a mist moving over a great salt marsh, to watch the flight of shore birds that have swept up and down the surf lines of the continents for untold thousands of years, to see the running of the old eels and the young shad to the sea, is to have knowledge of things that are as nearly eternal as any earthly life can be."

—RACHEL CARSON, *The Sea Around Us*

Job and Wilderness · *1997*

The first attempt of which I'm aware to answer the question: why are wild places valuable? comes in the Hebrew Bible, in the book of Job. Job, of course, suffers wretchedly and unfairly; he loses his family and his lands, and is reduced to lying in a dungheap at the edge of town, covered with oozing sores. Knowing that he had behaved justly, and puzzled at his travails, Job demands an audience with God—demands that God justify Himself. His is the first modern voice in the Bible, really in all of literature. And the answer that God, speaking from a whirl-wind, gives him is a curious one.

God says nothing about justice, about evenhandedness, about sin, about any of the current metaphysical categories that usually occupy our attention. Instead, He conducts a tour of the physical earth—its tides and storms and forests and waters, its magnificent animals. He speaks sarcastically some of the time, taunting Job with the man's insignificance: Where were you when I laid down the boundaries of the oceans? When I placed the very stars in the heavens? But He also speaks with great tenderness:

> Do you tell the antelope to calve
> or ease her when she is in labor?
> Do you count the months of her fullness
> and know when her time has come?
> She kneels; she tightens her womb;
> she pants, she presses, gives birth.

Her little ones grow up:
they leave and never return.

When Job asks why he must suffer, God talks about antelopes, vultures, lions, ostriches. God points out that it is He who cuts a path for the thunderstorm to "water the desolate wasteland, the land where no man lives, to make the wilderness blossom." The clear and overpowering implication of his speech—God's longest sustained speech in the whole Bible—is that Job and people in general are but a part of creation, not its central feature. Even our notions of justice fit into something very much larger and less tame.

I recite this story simply to say that one value wilderness has *for us* (clearly subsidiary to the many values it has for other creatures) is that it allows us to remember how big we are. We live, at the end of the twentieth century, in a world designed to constantly make us seem large and important. The television natters at us constantly about the importance of our desires; we can scarcely drive down a road in this country without a sign to flatter and cajole us. The marks of our power are everywhere about us, especially in the ways that we annihilate space and time through our technology.

Yet the marks of our infatuation are everywhere about us too, in a culture of instant gratification that descends easily into selfishness and violence. Wilderness is one of the few places (along with soup kitchens and hospitals and other places that transcendent human love can be practiced) that remind us there are other definitions of what it means to be a man or a woman. Wilderness allows us to entertain the possibility that instead of being constantly at the center of the world, we might be more comfortable as one part among many. In this way, it helps preserve a diversity of human identities just as it helps preserve a diversity of other creatures.

Most of my work deals with the largest environmental problems, forces like global climate change. The data convince me we will be unable to deal with these challenges until we manage to shift, subtly but powerfully, our estimation of how big, how central, how important we should be; until we find other ways of living that suit us better, and that suit the planet better as well. Wilderness [. . .] is a crucial schoolhouse for this transformation. A clearcut next to it would be the equivalent of a boombox blaring static in one corner of that schoolhouse. It would keep us from hearing the voice from the whirlwind, the voice from our heart, the voice that says we are a small part of something very wonderful and very right.

→>-<-

JACK TURNER
The Abstract Wild · 1996

The majority of Americans have no experience of the wild. We are surrounded by national parks, wilderness areas, wildlife preserves, sanctuaries, and refuges. We love to visit them. We also visit foreign parks and wilderness; we visit wild, exotic cultures. We are deluged with commercial images of wildness: coffee-table books, calendars, postcards, posters, T-shirts, and placemats. There are nature movies. A comprehensive bibliography of nature books would strain a small computer. There are hundreds of nature magazines with every conceivable emphasis: yuppie outdoor magazines, geographical magazines, philosophy magazines, scientific magazines, ecology magazines, and political magazines. Zoos and animal parks and marine lands abound, displaying a selection of beasts exceeded only by Noah's.

From this we conclude that modern man's knowledge and experience of wild nature is extensive. But it is not extensive. Rather, what we have is extensive experience of a severely diminished wilderness animal or place—a *caricature* of its former self; or, we have extensive indirect experience of wild nature via photographic images and the written word. This is not experience of the wild, not gross contact. [. . .]

When we deal in such abstractions boundaries are blurred, between the real and the fake, between the wild and the tame, between independent and dependent, between the original and the copy, between the healthy and the diminished. Blurring takes the edge off loss and removes us from our responsibilities. *Wild nature is not lost; we have collected it; you can go see it whenever you want.* With the aid of our infinite artifice this fake has replaced the natural. It's not really *very* different from the original! Why worry? As Umberto Eco observes in *Travels in Hyperreality,* "The ideology of this America wants to establish reassurance through imitation." And that ideology has succeeded; we are reassured, we are not angry, we are not even upset.

→>-<-

Wilderness is now—for much of North America—places that are formally set aside on public lands—Forest Service or Bureau of Land Management holdings or state and federal parks. Some tiny but critical tracts are held by private nonprofit groups like The Nature Conservancy or The Trust for Public Land. These are the shrines saved from all the land that was once known and lived on by the original people, the little bits left as they were, the last little places where intrinsic nature totally wails, blooms, nests, glints away. They make up only 2 percent of the land of the United States.

But wildness is not limited to the 2 percent formal wilderness areas. Shifting scales, it is everywhere: ineradicable populations of fungi, moss, mold, yeasts, and such that surround and inhabit us. Deer mice on the back porch, deer bounding across the freeway, pigeons in the park, spiders in the corners. There were crickets in the paint locker of the *Sappa Creek* oil tanker, as I worked as a wiper in the engine room out in mid-Pacific, cleaning brushes. Exquisite complex beings in their energy webs inhabiting the fertile corners of the urban world in accord with the rules of wild systems, the visible hardy stalks and stems of vacant lots and railroads, the persistent raccoon squads, bacteria in the loam and in our yogurt. The term *culture,* in its meaning of "a deliberately maintained aesthetic and intellectual life" and in its other meaning of "the totality of socially transmitted behavior patterns," is never far from a biological root meaning as in "yogurt culture"—a nourishing habitat. Civilization is permeable, and could be as inhabited as the wild is.

Wilderness may temporarily dwindle, but wildness won't go away. A ghost wilderness hovers around the entire planet: the millions of tiny seeds of the original vegetation are hiding in the mud on the foot of an arctic tern, in the dry desert sands, or in the wind. These seeds are each uniquely adapted to a specific soil or circumstance, each with its own little form and fluff, ready to float, freeze, or be swallowed, always preserving the germ. Wilderness will inevitably return, but it will not be as fine a world as the one that was glistening in the early morning of the Holocene. Much life will be lost in the wake of human agency on earth, that of the twentieth and twenty-first centuries. Much is already lost—the soils and waters unravel:

> "What's that dark thing in the water?
>   Is it not an oil-soaked otter?"

Where do we start to resolve the dichotomy of the civilized and the wild?

→►◄←

EVAN EISENBERG
The Ecology of Eden · 1998

We need pure wilderness. Our pure wildernesses should function, however, not as boxes, but as organs: hearts and lungs from which wildness circulates. So there must be arteries as well: corridors of wildness, underpassed or overpassed by the highways, allowing flora and fauna to migrate and expand. The network might embrace the wooded windbreaks of farms, city greenbelts, and disused railway rights-of-way as well as corridors created for the purpose. Like the hedgerows that once crisscrossed much of England—intricate living walls dense with trees, shrubs, small mammals, insects, and songbirds—such corridors would turn the walled garden inside out so that, like a Klein bottle, it would contain the universe. The wall between man and nature would fall, for the wall would be nature.

But even this would be an empty gesture if there were not also capillaries, branching and subbranching, touching nearly every cell of civilization with wildness. Just how this would work is harder to imagine the more encased we are in industrial life. . . . A lawn in Tucson sporting mesquite and bloodroot amaranth rather than water-guzzling grass; a Massachusetts home encircled with nut trees and berry bushes instead of privet and a tomato patch; a toilet that makes compost instead of sewage; city sewage treatment by willows, duckweed, snails, and microbes in narrow greenhouses running along the sidewalk. At this point, of course, the network would no longer be visible as a network. At this point wilderness would not be a thing or a place, but a process. [. . .]

For better or worse, our relation to nature can only be cultural. Nature is never just nature. A landscape—even a place that is utterly wild—is admired not only for itself, but for its links to previous human experience. Whig bankers tried to re-create classical landscapes not merely because they were pretty but because they were the proper backdrops for a heroic life. The vast emptinesses of the American West shimmer with the ghosts of cowboys and murdered Indians. Africa's savanna gains hardly more glamour from its lions and elephants than from the legendary white hunters who stalked them. Even an explorer who treads where no other human has trod inevitably sees the place as the kind of place where other explorers—his heroes—have gone. If one day humans scale the peaks of Mars, they will probably see the view from the top through the borrowed eyes of Edmund Hillary.

Every longing for nature is also a longing for some other culture. Wordsworth would lief be "a pagan suckled in a creed outworn." Nature was not the only book Thoreau read at Walden. Without the help of Homer, the Bible, and the Upanishads, the book of nature would have been unreadable. And there was the unwritten culture of the Indians to guide him— the mute arrowheads that "sprang from the ground when he touched it." Perched on the cliffs of Yosemite, Muir had his dog-eared Emerson; but exactly what culture did he admire? Or was he the harbinger of a truly cultureless love of nature— the love of pure wilderness, excluding all humans? The love that has no consequences for our way of life, that is therefore a dead end? [. . .]

The dream of a direct relation to nature is a foolish one for society as a whole, yet when certain individuals act on it— when they go into the wilderness determined to meet it face to face—they may come back with wisdom that everyone can use. Thoreau, John Muir, Bob Marshall, Edward Abbey, Annie

Dillard, Edward Hoagland, Gary Snyder: try to imagine them anywhere but in America. (You might be able to imagine them in another frontier country, like New Zealand—but France or Germany? Not a chance.) Whether they come back convinced that a direct relation to nature is impossible or that it is the only thing worth achieving on earth, they give us something we desperately need to chew on: the problem of understanding nature on its own terms. Their visions have helped bring about the preservation of vast tracts of wilderness and near wilderness. And though putting wilderness in boxes is not enough, it is a necessary start.

→>-<←

DONALD WORSTER
The Wilderness of History · 1997

The wilderness has been a symbol of freedom for many people, and it is a primordial as well as cultural sense of freedom that they have sought. Freedom, it must be granted, can become another word for irresponsibility. Yet almost always the preservation of wilderness freedom in the United States has been interwoven with a counterbalancing principle of moral restraint. In fact, this linkage of freedom and restraint may be the most important feature of the wilderness movement. Those 100 million acres exist not only as a place where evolution can continue on its own terms, where we humans can take refuge from our technological creations, but also as a place where we can learn the virtue of restraint: this far we drive, plow, mine, cut, and no farther.

Old-time religions enforced moral restraint on their follow-ers by the practice of tithing, a practice that has almost com-pletely disappeared under the impact of the market revolution. But the practice of tithing is too good an idea to lose. Without saying so, we have created in the form of wilderness a new, more secular form of the ancient religious tithe. We have set aside a small portion of the country as the part we return to the earth that supports us, the earth that was here before any of us. We are not yet up to a full tithe, but we are still working on it.

A place of restraint as well as a place of freedom for all liv-ing things, the wilderness has promoted, I believe, a broader ethic of environmental responsibility all across this nation. Far from being an indefensible obsession, wilderness preservation has been one of our most noble achievements as a people. With no broad claims to American exceptionalism, I will say that here is a model of virtuous action for other societies to study and emulate. This is not to say that historians have been wrong to criticize weaknesses in the wilderness movement. They have only been wrong when they have denigrated the movement as a whole, carelessly encouraged its enemies, and made bad historical arguments. The real danger we face as a nation, we should remember, is not loving wilderness too much but loving our pocketbooks more.

→>-<-

There is a place where the sidewalk ends
And before the street begins
And there the grass grows soft and white,
And there the sun burns crimson bright.
And there the moon-bird rests from his flight
To cool in the peppermint wind.

Let us leave this place where the smoke blows black
And the dark street winds and bends.
Past the pits where the asphalt flowers grow
We shall walk with a walk that is measured and slow,
And watch where the chalk-white arrows go
To the place where the sidewalk ends.
Yes we'll walk with a walk that is measured and slow,
And we'll go where the chalk-white arrows go
For the children, they mark, and the children, they know
The place where the sidewalk ends.

"What freedom means is freedom to choose. What civilization means is some sense of how to choose and from among what options. [. . .] We need to learn to listen to the land, hear what it says, understand what it can and can't do over the long haul; what, especially in the west, it should not be asked to do. To learn such things, we have to have access to natural wild land."

—WALLACE STEGNER, *The Gift of Wilderness*

"Afterward, a Kenyan friend, Wangari Waigwa-stone, and I spoke about darkness and stars. 'I was raised under an African sky,' she said. 'Darkness was never something I was afraid of. The clarity, definition, and profusion of stars became maps as to how one navigates at night. I always knew where I was simply by looking up.' She paused. 'My sons do not have these guides. They have no relationship to darkness. Nothing in their imagination tells them there are pathways in the night they can move through.'"

—TERRY TEMPEST WILLIAMS, *Refuge*

Chapter 5: People and Nature Together

"We are all indigenous to this planet, this mosaic of wild gardens we are being called by nature and history to reinhabit in good spirit. Part of the responsibility is to choose a place. To restore the land one must live and work in a place. To work in a place is to work with others. People who work together in a place become a community, and a community, in time, grows culture. To work on behalf of the wild is to restore culture."

—GARY SNYDER, *Rediscovery of Turtle Island*

-+->-<-+-

MICHAEL POLLAN
Second Nature · 1991

A pedestrian standing at the corner of Houston Street and LaGuardia Place in Manhattan might think that the wilderness had reclaimed a tiny corner of the city's grid here. Ten years ago, an environmental artist persuaded the city to allow him to create on this site a "time landscape" showing New Yorkers what Manhattan looked like before the white man arrived. On a small hummock he planted oak, hickory, maples, junipers, and sassafras, and they've grown up to form a nearly impenetrable tangle, which is protected from New Yorkers by the steel bars of a fence now thickly embroidered with vines. It's exactly the sort of "garden" of which Emerson and Thoreau would have approved—for the very reason that it's *not* a garden. Or at least that's the conceit.

I walk by this anti-garden most mornings on my way to work, and for some reason it has always irritated me. It adjoins a lively community garden, where any summer evening will find a handful of neighborhood people busy cultivating their little patches of flowers and vegetables. Next to this display of enterprise, the untended "time landscape" makes an interesting foil. But the juxtaposition has always struck me as pat, just a shade too righteous, and walking by one day last summer I figured out why.

My mind fixed on the weeds just then hoisting their flags of victory over my garden, I recognized one of the vines twining along the fence from the field guides I'd been consulting. It was nightshade, a species, I recalled—and not without my own sweet pang of righteousness—that is not indigenous: it came to America with the white man. Aha! This smug little wilderness was really a garden after all. Unless somebody weeds it, sedu-lously and knowledgeably, it will quickly be overrun with alien species. This "time landscape" is in perpetual danger of degen-erating into an everyday vacant lot; only a gardener, armed with a hoe and a set of "invidious distinctions," can save it.

Once, of course, this would not have been the case. But that was a long time ago; by now, we have made so many changes in the land that some form of gardening has become unavoid-able, even in those places we wish to preserve as monuments to our absence. This, it seems to me, is one of the lessons of the massive fires in Yellowstone in 1988. At a certain point in history, doing nothing is not necessarily benign. Since 1972, park management in Yellowstone has followed a policy called "natural burn," under which naturally occurring fires are allowed to burn freely—before 1972, every fire was put out immediately. All those years of fire fighting left an abundance of volatile dead wood on the forest floor and that may be why, when the fires finally came in the drought year of 1988, they proved so catastrophic. Yellowstone's ecosystem having already been altered by the earlier policy of fire suppression, the new policy could not in any real sense be "natural"; nor were the fires it fostered.

There's no going back. Even Yellowstone, our country's greatest "wilderness," stands in need of careful management —it's too late to simply "leave it alone." I have no idea what the best fire policy for Yellowstone might be, but I do know that men and women, armed with scientific knowledge and acting through human institutions, will have to choose and then implement one. In doing so, they will have to grapple with the fact that, long before Yellowstone was declared a "wilderness area," Indians were setting fires in it; were these "natural"? If the goal is to restore Yellowstone to its pre-Columbian condition, their policy may well have to include the setting of fires. They will also have to decide how many tourists Yellowstone can support, whether wolves should be reintroduced to keep the elk population from exploding, and a host of other complicated questions. Today, even Yellowstone must be "gardened."

A century after Thoreau wrote that "in wildness is the preservation of the world," Wendell Berry, the Kentucky poet and farmer, added a corollary that would have made no sense at all to Thoreau, and yet that is necessary. Berry wrote that "in human culture is the preservation of wildness." I take him to mean that it's too late now to do nothing. Only human wisdom and forbearance can save places like Yellowstone.

Thoreau, and his many heirs among contemporary naturalists and radical environmentalists, assume that human culture is the problem, not the solution. So they urge us to shed our anthropocentrism and learn to live among other species as equals. This sounds like a fine, ecological idea, until you realize that the earth would be even worse off if we started behaving any more like animals than we already do. The survival strategy of most species is to extend their dominion as far and as brutally as they can, until they run up against some equally brutal natural limit that checks their progress. Isn't this exactly what we've been doing?

What sets us apart from other species is culture, and what is culture but forbearance? Conscience, ethical choice, memory, discrimination: it is these very human and decidedly unecological faculties that offer the planet its last best hope. It is true that, historically, we've concentrated on exercising these faculties in the human rather than the natural estate, but that doesn't mean they *cannot* be exercised there. Indeed, this is the work that now needs to be done: to bring more culture to our conduct in nature, not less.

If I seem to have wandered far afield of weeds, consider what weeding is: the process by which we make informed choices in nature, discriminate between good and bad, apply our intelligence and sweat to the earth. To weed is to bring culture to nature—which is why we say, when we are weeding, that we are *cultivating* the soil. Weeding, in this sense, is not a nuisance that follows from gardening, but its very essence.

And, like gardening, weeding at a certain point becomes an obligation. As I learned in my flower bed, mere neglect won't bring back "nature."

In this, my yard is not so different from the rest of the world. We cannot live in it without changing nature irrevocably; having done so, we're obliged to tend to the consequences of the changes we've wrought, which is to say, to weed. "Weeding" is what will save places like Yellowstone, but only if we recognize that weeding is not just something we do to the land—only if we recognize the need to cultivate our *own* nature, too. For though we may be the earth's gardeners, we are also its weeds. And we won't get anywhere until we come to terms with this crucial ambiguity about our role—that we are at once the problem and the only possible solution to the problem.

"In a culture that views ecology as the antithesis to economy, it is difficult to think clearly about how we live in relation to where we are. So we drop the subject from the political debate entirely. We have witnessed the collapse of the communist economic system with a strange smugness, unaware that our own vaunted way of life is in the process of bankrupting us, too. Even environmentalists, committed to the rescue of wild places, have failed to address the problem of human ecology in the places we live and work."

—JAMES HOWARD KUNSTLER, *The Geography of Nowhere*

GENE LOGSDON
The Contrary Farmer · *1993*

It is in the garden that we get down on our hands and knees and feel the soil draw us into an understanding of the interrelationships between all living things. One generality that comes close to being always true in my experience is that farmers who do not garden or who have never gardened, tend to be insensitive to the biological nature of their work and therefore inattentive to all nature including human nature. Urbanites who do not garden are even worse in this regard since they have no frame of reference at all for coming to grips with the realities of biology. They not only don't understand what farmers are up against, but cannot see that these problems are everybody's concern.

On the other hand, the more gardeners immerse themselves in their biological art, the more they not only understand farmers but become farmers—nurturers of life. Indeed, no matter how small the garden, even as small as a miniature planting of mosses inside a gallon jar, the biological activity going on there is a microcosm of the farm.

It seems to me that the garden is the only practical way for urban societies to come in *close* contact with the basic realities of life, and if that contact is not close, it is not meaningful at all. To feel the searing heat as well as the comforting warmth of the sun, or to endure the dry wind as well as the soothing breeze; to pray for rain but not too much rain; to long for a spate of dry weather but not too long; to listen to the music of nature as well as the rock beat of human culture; to know that life depends on eating and being eaten; to accept the decay of death as the only way to achieve the resurrection of life; to realize that diversification of species, not multiplication within a species, is the responsibility of rational intelligence—nature will handle that latter activity much better than we can; to grow in personal simplicity while appreciating biological complexity, so that in the garden there is time to sit and think, to produce good food for the mind—these are all part of an education that the industrial world hungers for but cannot name.

✦✦✦

WENDELL BERRY
Another Turn of the Crank · *1995*

Thirty years ago, one of the organizations leading the fight against strip mining was the Appalachian Group to Save the Land and the People. This seemed an exemplary organization —an informed local response to a local calamity—and I was strongly affected and influenced by it. What most impressed me was the complexity of purpose announced in its name: it proposed to save the land *and* the people. This seems to me still an inescapable necessity. You really cannot specialize the work of conservation. You cannot save the land apart from the people or the people apart from the land. To save either, you must save both—that is a lesson taught nowhere better than in the economic history of the Commonwealth of Kentucky. To save both the land and the people, you need a strong rural economy.

In truth, you need several strong rural economies, for even so small a state as ours has many regions, and a good economy joins local people conservingly to their local landscapes.

If we are serious about conservation, then we are going to have to quit thinking of our work as a sequence of specialized and temporary responses to a sequence of specialized and temporary emergencies. We will have to realize finally that our work is economic. We are going to have to come up with competent, practical, at-home answers to the humblest human questions: How should we live? How should we keep house? How should we provide ourselves with food, clothing, shelter, heat, light, learning, amusement, rest? How, in short, ought we to use the world?

+>-<+

MURRAY BOOKCHIN
The Ecology of Freedom · *1982*

In the Norse legends, Odin, to obtain wisdom, drinks of the magic fountain that nourishes the World Tree. In return, the god must forfeit one of his eyes. The symbolism, here, is clear: Odin must pay a penalty for acquiring the insight that gives him a measure of control over the natural world and breaches its pristine harmony. But his "wisdom" is that of a one-eyed man. Although he sees the world more acutely, his vision is one-sided. The "wisdom" of Odin involves a renunciation not only of what Josef Weber has called the "primordial bond with nature," but also of the honesty of perception that accords with nature's early unity. Truth achieves exactness, predictability, and above all, manipulability; it becomes science in the customary sense of the term. But science as we know it today is the fragmented one-sided vision of a one-eyed god, whose vantage-point entails domination and antagonism, not coequality and harmony. In the Norse legends, this "wisdom" leads to Ragnarok, the downfall of the gods and the destruction of the tribal world. In our day, this one-sided "wisdom" is laden with the prospects of nuclear immolation and ecological catastrophe.

Humanity has passed through a long history of one-sidedness and of a social condition that has always contained the potential of destruction, despite its creative achievements in technology. The great project of our time must be to open the other eye: to see all-sidedly and wholly, to heal and transcend the cleavage between humanity and nature that came with early wisdom. Nor can we deceive ourselves that the reopened eye will be focused on the visions and myths of primordial peoples, for history has labored over thousands of years to produce entirely new domains of reality that enter into our very humanness. Our capacity for freedom—which includes our capacity for individuality, experience, and desire—runs deeper than that of our distant progenitors. We have established a broader material basis for free time, play, security, perception, and sensuousness—a material potentiality for broader domains of freedom and humanness—than humanity in a primordial bond with nature could possibly achieve.

But we cannot remove our bonds unless we know them. However unconscious its influence may be, a legacy of domination permeates our thinking, values, emotions, indeed our very musculature. History dominates us all the more when we are ignorant of it. The historic unconscious must be made conscious. Cutting across the very legacy of domination is another: the legacy of freedom that lives in the daydreams of humanity, in the great ideals and movements—rebellious, anarchic, and Dionysian—that have welled up in all great eras of social transition. In our own time, these legacies are intertwined like strands and subvert the clear patterns that existed in the past, until the language of freedom becomes interchangeable with that of domination. This confusion has been the tragic fate of modern socialism, a doctrine that has been bled of all its generous ideals. Thus, the past must be dissected in order to exorcise it and to acquire a new integrity of vision. We must reexamine the cleavages that separated humanity from nature, and the splits within the human community that originally produced this cleavage, if the concept of wholeness is to become intelligible and the reopened eye to glimpse a fresh image of freedom.

→>–<+

GARY PAUL NABHAN
Cultures of Habitat · 1997

Conservationists have again and again tried to build "an ark for biodiversity." Like Noah, they have been willing to usher along every kind of plant and animal as long as no other *peoples* are given a place aboard the ark, forgetting that until the very moment of crisis, a diversity of cultures served to safeguard that biodiversity. The Huaorani, Tukano, and Zaparta have not been offered berths to ensure their own survival. Conservationists have given them little place in their plans except as bystanders, allowed to watch as all the animals go two by two up to higher ground.

It is ironic how many conservationists have presumed that biodiversity can survive where indigenous cultures have been displaced or at least disrupted from practicing their traditional land-management strategies. Ironic because most biodiversity remaining on earth today occurs in areas where cultural diversity also persists. Of the nine countries in which 60 percent of the world's remaining 6,500 languages are spoken, six of them are also centers of megadiversity for flora and fauna: Mexico, Brazil, Indonesia, India, Zaire, and Australia. Geographer David Harmon has made lists of the twenty-five countries harboring the greatest number of endemic wildlife species within their boundaries and of the twenty-five countries where the greatest number of endemic languages are spoken. Those two lists have sixteen countries in common. It is fair to say that wherever many cultures have coexisted within the same region, biodiversity has also survived.

Let me state this principle as a negative correlation, like a scratchboard etching: wherever empires have spread to suppress other cultures' languages and land-tenure traditions, the loss of biodiversity has been dramatic. Civilizations that conquer other cultures and force them to adopt extensive grain agriculture or livestock grazing are particularly taxing on regionally restricted floras and faunas. With colonists at the helm, arks inevitably sink.

David Harmon has wondered why, despite these significant correlations between the distributions of biodiversity hot spots and linguistically rich cultural areas, some conservation biologists still don't see the survival of cultural diversity as related to their own concerns. If such biologists are typically attracted to E. O. Wilson's "biophilia hypothesis"—that humans have an intrinsic need for meaningful contact with other life-forms—then why, he asks, do they not necessarily assume that we have a hard-wired predilection for *cross-cultural* contact: "I suppose that we are waiting for a cultural analog of the biophilia hypothesis, one which does not merely claim that cultural diversity is 'interesting' but one which explains why contact with cultural diversity makes us fully human."

→>‹←

EVAN EISENBERG
The Ecology of Eden · *1998*

Some say we ought not to grieve overmuch for the loss of biodiversity, since our own cultural diversity is just as good. But cultural diversity will not keep the rain falling or the gases of the atmosphere in balance. Moreover, cultural diversity is itself dependent on biological diversity.

As I sit at my desk, snow is falling outside; Sibelius is playing on the stereo inside. As plainly as snow is born of clouds is this music born of snow. From the spruce forests of Finland to the red deserts of Australia, every landscape in which humans have lived has sent up its characteristic shoots of song. Conversely, every novel, poem, painting, and play has roots, at however many removes, in a landscape (or in several). One need not swallow whole the doctrine of environmental determinism to see that it has a kernel of truth.

As natural diversity has been plowed under, cultural diversity has gone down with it. This was true in Sumerian times and it is true today. But it has not always been evident. As peoples mingle and empires stretch their limbs, it looks for a while as if diversity—both natural and cultural—were increasing. Tigers and hyenas appear in the heart of Rome; legionnaires are inducted into the mysteries of Isis and Mithra. Even in the newly conquered provinces there is a flurry of novelty, as statues of Augustus take their place beside those of Ra. If you count the hothouse plants of the New York Botanical Garden and the vegetables dished out in Asian restaurants, you may conclude that the biodiversity of New York City is greater now than it was when Peter Stuyvesant debarked. Arguably, the city's cultural diversity is greater than that of any like-sized parcel of land in history. But how long can this last? When New York has tightened its grasp on Thailand and Nigeria—when American TV and American hybrid seeds have done their work—how much that is truly Thai or truly Hausa will be left to enrich New York? [. . .]

Thanks to free trade, man-made landscapes that have evolved for centuries—cultures in the most ancient sense, upon which cultures in the broader sense are founded—are vanishing almost as quickly as natural ecosystems. Small mixed farms go under, replaced by factory farms producing the single crop that can be grown more cheaply here than anywhere else. In wealthy regions, farming often vanishes altogether, replaced by industry or by residential development.

We are squeezing the whole world into a single ecosystem, a single market, and a single culture. American prairie grasses must compete with European grasses; farmers in India must compete with farmers in Australia; moviemakers in Turkey must compete with Hollywood. True, differences in climate and soil will keep every forest in the world from looking exactly like every other forest; differences of language and faith will, for a time at least, have a similar effect in the cultural realm. But that is not to say that the forests will be healthy forests or the cultures healthy cultures.

A planetary culture that is good for the planet is a hard thing to imagine. No matter how pious its intentions, it cannot possibly know what is best for each part of the planet. Yet one is just as hard put to imagine how the spread of a planetary culture could be stopped. Woman and man have tasted the fruit of cosmopolitanism, a fruit that tastes like Anjou pear on Monday, kiwi on Tuesday, lichee nut on Wednesday, and Cape gooseberry on Thursday. It is a taste that is easily acquired.

No one has the right to stop people from being Westernized or cosmopolitanized if they choose to be. But there are many people on earth who do not so choose, but are forced. Land is taken from traditional small farmers and amassed in plantations. Local elites are, in effect, bribed to extend the world market and the cash economy into places that want neither. Loggers, ranchers, miners, oil drillers, and settlers level and scorch and scar other people's habitat: and the loss of habitat is something which cultural diversity no more than natural diversity can long survive. Nor is free trade a law of nature which only flat-earthers would resist. It is deliberately imposed by global elites on people who, given the choice, would rather protect their traditional landscape and way of life.

Maybe we flatter ourselves when we assume that the first glimpse of a television set or snort from a can of Coke must turn any sentient being into an addict of Western pop culture and consumerism. Those photons and those bubbles are powerful things, to be sure—especially when the photons spend half their time insisting that life without the bubbles is not worth living. But so is the breath of the forest; so is the voice of the ancestors.

The analogies I have been drawing between nature, culture, and economics must not be pushed too far. An ecologist speaking of invasive exotics—saying that they are tough, that they outcompete the natives, that they don't play by the rules, that they can destroy in a few decades a system that has taken millennia to evolve—often sounds like a bigot talking about Jews or Asians. But the ecologist's statements are based mainly on fact, while the bigot's are based on rumor, fear, and frustration. All humans are members of a single species. Human cultures (and for that matter, human "races") are not, like species, distinct entities; they are fluid and have mingled fluidly from the earliest times of which we have any knowledge. Syncretism has always been a prime source of cultural energy. My point is simply that the energy it releases is energy stored over centuries of relative isolation: and my fear is that the great explosion we are now seeing may end in cultural heat-death.

→>-<←

After more than thirty years I have at last arrived at the candor necessary to stand on this part of the earth that is so full of my own history and so much damaged by it, and ask: What *is* this place? What is in it? What is its nature? How should men live in it? What must I do?

I have not found the answers, though I believe that in partial and fragmentary ways they have begun to come to me. But the questions are more important than their answers. In the final sense they *have* no answers. They are like the questions—they are perhaps the same questions—that were the discipline of Job. They are a part of the necessary enactment of humility, teaching a man what his importance is, what his responsibility is, and what his place is, both on the earth and in the order of things. And though the answers must always come obscurely and in fragments, the questions must be asked. They are fertile questions. In their implications and effects, they are moral and aesthetic and, in the best and fullest sense, practical. They promise a relationship to the world that is decent and preserving.

They are also, both in origin and effect, religious. I am uneasy with the term, for such religion as has been openly practiced in this part of the world has promoted and fed upon a destructive schism between body and soul, Heaven and earth. It has encouraged people to believe that the world is of no importance, and that their only obligation in it is to submit to certain churchly formulas in order to get to heaven. And so the people who might have been expected to care most selflessly for the world have had their minds turned elsewhere—to a pursuit of "salvation" that was really only another form of gluttony and self-love, the desire to perpetuate their lives beyond the life of the world. The Heaven-bent have abused the earth thoughtlessly, by inattention, and their negligence has permitted and encouraged others to abuse it deliberately. Once the creator was removed from the creation, divinity became only a remote abstraction, a social weapon in the hands of the religious institutions. This split in public values produced or was accompanied by, as it was bound to be, an equally artificial and ugly division in people's lives, so that a man, while pursuing Heaven with the sublime appetite he thought of as his soul, could turn his heart against his neighbors and his hands against the world. For these reasons, though I know that my questions *are* religious, I dislike having to *say* that they are.

"Adam was put in the garden 'to work it and protect it.' The two jobs are complementary, but they are also contradictory. From what are we to protect Eden, if not from our own work? The more we work the earth—by which I mean not only tilling but the whole spectrum of human meddling, from setting grass fires to splitting the atom—the more we are obliged to protect it. If we fail to do either, we fail to be fully human."

—EVAN EISENBERG, *The Ecology of Eden*

Henry David Thoreau
Walden · *1849*

There is commonly sufficient space about us. Our horizon is never quite at our elbows. The thick wood is not just at our door, nor the pond, but somewhat is always clearing, familiar and worn by us, appropriated and fenced in some way, and reclaimed from Nature. For what reason have I this vast range and circuit, some square miles of unfrequented forest, for my privacy, abandoned to me by men? My nearest neighbor is a mile distant, and no house is visible from any place but the hill-tops within half a mile of my own. I have my horizon bounded by woods all to myself; a distant view of the railroad where it touches the pond on the one hand, and of the fence which skirts the woodland road on the other. But for the most part it is as solitary where I live as on the prairies. It is as much Asia or Africa as New England. I have, as it were, my own sun and moon and stars, and a little world all to myself. At night there was never a traveller passed my house, or knocked at my door, more than if I were the first or last man; unless it were in the spring, when at long intervals some came from the village to fish for pouts,—they plainly fished much more in the Walden Pond of their own natures, and baited their hooks with darkness,—but they soon retreated, usually with light baskets, and left "the world to darkness and to me," and the black kernel of the night was never profaned by any human neighborhood. I believe that men are generally still a little afraid of the dark, though the witches are all hung, and Christianity and candles have been introduced.

Yet I experienced sometimes that the most sweet and tender, the most innocent and encouraging society may be found in any natural object, even for the poor misanthrope and most melancholy man. There can be no very black melancholy to him who lives in the midst of nature and has his senses still. There was never yet such a storm but it was Aeolian music to a healthy and innocent ear. Nothing can rightly compel a simple and brave man to a vulgar sadness. While I enjoy the friendship of the seasons I trust that nothing can make life a burden to me. The gentle rain which waters my beans and keeps me in the house to-day is not drear and melancholy, but good for me too. Though it prevents my hoeing them, it is of far more worth than my hoeing. If it should continue so long as to cause the seeds to rot in the ground and destroy the potatoes in the low lands, it would still be good for the grass on the uplands, and, being good for the grass, it would be good for me. Sometimes, when I compare myself with other men, it seems as if I were more favored by the gods than they, beyond any deserts that I am conscious of; as if I had a warrant and surety at their hands which my fellows have not, and were especially guided and guarded. I do not flatter myself, but if it be possible they flatter me. I have never felt lonesome, or in the least oppressed by a sense of solitude, but once, and that was a few weeks after I came to the woods, when, for an hour, I doubted if the near neighborhood of man was not essential to a serene and healthy life. To be alone was something unpleasant. But I was at the same time conscious of a slight insanity in my mood, and seemed to foresee my recovery. In the midst of a gentle rain while these thoughts prevailed, I was suddenly sensible of such sweet and beneficent society in Nature, in the very pattering of the drops, and in every sound and sight around my house, an infinite and unaccountable friendliness all at once like an atmosphere sustaining me, as made the fancied advantages of human neighborhood insignificant, and I have never thought of them since. Every little pine needle expanded and swelled with sympathy and befriended me. I was so distinctly made aware of the presence of something kindred to me, even in scenes which we are accustomed to call wild and dreary, and also that the nearest of blood to me and humanest was not a person nor a villager, that I thought no place could ever be strange to me again.

→>-<←

"An enduring agriculture must never cease to consider and respect and preserve wildness. The farm can exist only within the wilderness of mystery and natural force. And if the farm is to last and remain in health, the wilderness must survive within the farm. That is what agricultural fertility is: the survival of natural process in the human order."

—Wendell Berry, *The Unsettling of America*

III : TOWARD A NEW LAND ETHIC

The remaining chapters offer the land ethic response to the conditions of our world and of our movement. These are simple lessons which address our everyday existence: how we work and live and the stories we choose to tell our children. Each chapter examines how, in this increasingly specialized and interest-based world, land conservation can teach positive values about how people may live in a new way on this planet.

Chapter 6: Good Work

The conservation movement is quick to talk about place, but is often silent on work. And yet, the places we live and the work we do forge much of our beliefs. Good work is fundamental to the human experience and, therefore, a necessary component of any conservation philosophy that hopes to create a new land ethic. Whether we are farmers on the land or lawyers in an office tower, whatever work we do ultimately affects the land, and, therefore, our own consciousness. In this important sense, no one is divorced from the land and all share equally in its future. When deed and creed become aligned, all work takes on great material and spiritual value.

What difference does the quality of work make to an individual's and community's sense of worth? How might work complement the values of land conservation, and vice versa? In imagining a world defined by a shared land ethic, how might all types of work reinforce people's connection to the land? What is the role of land conservation in helping people to find good work in their lives?

Richard White
Do You Work for a Living? · *1995*

When [Bill] McKibben writes about his work, he comments that his office and the mountain he views from it are separate parts of his life. They are unconnected. In the office he is in control; outside he is not. Beyond his office window is nature, separate and independent. This is a clean division. Work and nature stand segregated and clearly distinguished.

I, like McKibben, type at a keyboard. On this clear June day I can see the Olympic Mountains in the distance. Like McKibben, I do modern work. I sort, compile, analyze, and organize. My bodily movement becomes electrical signals where my fingers intersect with a machine. Lights flicker on a screen. I expend little energy; I don't sweat, or ache, or grow physically tired. I produce at the end of this day no tangible product; there are only stored memories encoded when my fingers touched keys. There is no dirt or death or even consciousness of bodily labor when I am done. Trees still grow, animals still graze, fish still swim.

But, unlike McKibben, I cannot see my labor as separate from the mountains, and I know that my labor is not truly disembodied. If I sat and typed here day after day, as clerical workers type, without frequent breaks to wander and to look at the mountains, I would become achingly aware of my body. I might develop carpal tunnel syndrome. My body, the nature in me, would rebel. The lights on this screen need electricity, and this particular electricity comes from dams on the Skagit or Columbia. These dams kill fish; they alter the rivers that come from the Rockies, Cascades, and Olympics. The electricity they produce depends on the great seasonal cycles of the planet: on falling snow, melting waters, flowing rivers. In the end, these electrical impulses will take tangible form on paper from trees. Nature, altered and changed, is in this room. But this is masked. I type. I kill nothing. I touch no living thing. I seem to alter nothing but the screen. If I don't think about it, I can seem benign, the mountains separate and safe from me as the Adirondacks seem safe from McKibben as he writes his essays for the *New Yorker*. But, of course, the natural world has changed and continues to change to allow me to sit here, just as it changes to allow McKibben to write. My separation is an illusion. What is disguised is that I—unlike loggers, farmers, fishers, or herders—do not have to face what I alter, and so I learn nothing from it. The connection my labor makes flows in only one direction.

My work, I suspect, is similar to that of most environmentalists. Because it seems so distant from nature, it escapes the condemnation that the work that takes place out there, in "nature," attracts. I regularly read the *High Country News,* and its articles just as regularly denounce mining, ranching, and logging for the very real harm they do. And since the paper's editors have some sympathy for rural people trying to live on the land, letters from readers denounce the paper for not condemning these activities enough. The intention of those who defend old growth or denounce overgrazing is not to denounce hard physical work, but that is, in effect, what the articles do. There are few articles or letters denouncing university professors or computer programmers or accountants or lawyers for sullying the environment, although it is my guess that a single lawyer or accountant could, on a good day, put the efforts of Paul Bunyan to shame.

Most humans must work, and our work—all our work—inevitably embeds us in nature, including what we consider wild and pristine places. Environmentalists have invited the kind of attack contained in the Forks bumper sticker by identifying nature with leisure, by masking the environmental consequences of their own work. To escape it, and perhaps even to find allies among people unnecessarily made into enemies, there has to be some attempt to come to terms with work. Work does not prevent harm to the natural world—Forks itself is evidence of that—but if work is not perverted into a means of turning place into property, it can teach us how deeply our work and nature's work are intertwined.

And if we do not come to terms with work, if we fail to pursue the implications of our labor and our bodies in the natural world, then we will return to patrolling the borders. We will turn public lands into a public playground; we will equate wild lands with rugged play; we will imagine nature as an escape, a place where we are born again. It will be a paradise where we leave work behind. Nature may turn out to look a lot like an organic Disneyland, except it will be harder to park.

There is, too, an inescapable corollary to this particular piece of self-deception. We will condemn ourselves to spending most of our lives outside of nature, for there can be no permanent place for us inside. Having demonized those whose very lives recognize the tangled complexity of a planet in which we kill, destroy and alter as a condition of living and working, we can claim an innocence that in the end is merely irresponsibility.

If, on the other hand, environmentalism could focus on our work rather than on our leisure, then a whole series of fruitful new angles on the world might be possible. It links us to each other, and it links us to nature. It unites issues as diverse as workplace safety and grazing on public lands; it unites toxic sites and wilderness areas. In taking responsibility for our own lives and work, in unmasking the connections of our labor and nature's labor, in giving up our hopeless fixation on purity, we may ultimately find a way to break the borders that imprison nature as much as ourselves. Work, then, is where we should begin.

→>-<←

WENDELL BERRY
Conservation Is Good Work · 1992

No settled family or community has ever called its home place an "environment." None has ever called its feeling for its home place "biocentric" or "anthropocentric." None has ever thought of its connection to its home place as "ecological," deep or shallow. The concepts and insights of the ecologists are of great usefulness in our predicament, and we can hardly escape the need to speak of "ecology" and "ecosystems." But the terms themselves are culturally sterile. They come from the juiceless, abstract intellectuality of the universities which was invented to disconnect, displace, and disembody the mind. The real names of the environment are the names of rivers and river valleys; creeks, ridges, and mountains; towns and cities; lakes, woodlands, lanes, roads, creatures, and people.

And the real name of our connection to this everywhere different and differently named earth is "work." We are connected by work even to the places where we don't work, for all places are connected; it is clear by now that we cannot exempt one place from our ruin of another. The name of our *proper* connection to the earth is "good work," for good work involves much giving of honor. It honors the source of its materials; it honors the place where it is done; it honors the art by which it is done; it honors the thing that it makes and the user of the made thing. Good work is always modestly scaled, for it cannot ignore either the nature of individual places or the differences between places, and it always involves a sort of religious humility, for not everything is known. Good work can be defined only in particularity, for it must be defined a little differently for every one of the places and every one of the workers on the earth.

The name of our present society's connection to the earth is "bad work"—work that is only generally and crudely defined, that enacts a dependence that is ill understood, that enacts no affection and gives no honor. Every one of us is to some extent guilty of this bad work. This guilt does not mean that we must indulge in a lot of breast-beating and confession; it means only that there is much good work to be done by every one of us and that we must begin to do it. All of us are responsible for bad work, not so much because we do it ourselves (though we all do it) as because we have it done for us by other people.

→>⤙←

E. F. SCHUMACHER
Good Work · *1979*

A recent article in the London *Times* began with these words: "Dante, when composing his visions of hell, might well have included the mindless, repetitive boredom of working on a factory assembly line. It destroys initiative and rots brains, yet millions of British workers are committed to it for most of their lives." The remarkable thing is that this statement, like countless similar ones made before it, aroused no interest: there were no hot denials or anguished agreements; no reactions at all. The strong and terrible words—"visions of hell," "destroys initiative and rots brains," and so on—attracted no reprimand that they were misstatements or overstatements, that they were irresponsible or hysterical exaggerations or subversive propaganda; no, people read them, sighed and nodded, I suppose, and moved on. Not even the ecologists, conservationists, and doomwatchers are interested in this matter. If someone had asserted that certain man-made arrangements destroyed the initiative and rotted the brains of millions of birds or seals or wild animals in the game reserves of Africa, such an assertion would have been either refuted or accepted as a serious challenge. If someone had asserted that not the minds and brains of millions of workers were being rotted but their bodies, again there would have been considerable interest. After all, there are safety regulations, inspectors, claims for damages, and so forth. No management is unaware of its duty to avoid accidents or physical conditions which impair workers' health. But workers' brains, minds, and souls are a different matter.

A recent semiofficial report, submitted by the British government to the Stockholm Conference, bears the title "Natural Resources: Sinews for Survival." The most important of all resources are obviously the initiative, imagination, and brainpower of man himself. We all know this and are ready to devote very substantial funds to what we call education. So, if the problem is "survival," one might fairly expect to find some discussion relating to the preservation and, if possible, the development of the most precious of all natural resources, human brains. However, such expectations are not fulfilled. "Sinews for Survival" deals with all the material factors—minerals, energy, water, etc.—but not at all with such immaterial resources as initiative, imagination, and brainpower.

Considering the centrality of work in human life, one might have expected that every textbook on economics, sociology, politics, and related subjects would present a theory of work as one of the indispensable foundation stones for all further expositions. After all, it is work which occupies most of the energies of the human race, and what people actually *do* is normally more important, for understanding them, than what they say, or what they spend their money on, or what they own, or how they vote. A person's work is undoubtedly one of the most decisive formative influences on his character and personality. However, the truth of the matter is that we look in vain for any presentations of theories of work in these textbooks. The question of what the work does to the worker is hardly ever asked, not to mention the question of whether the real task might not be to adapt the work to the needs of the worker rather than to demand that the worker adapt himself to the needs of the work—which means, of course, primarily to the needs of the machine.

Let us ask then: How does work relate to the end and purpose of man's being? It has been recognized in all authentic teachings of mankind that every human being born into this world has to work not merely to keep himself alive but to strive toward perfection. To keep himself alive, he needs various goods and services, which will not be forthcoming without human labor. To perfect himself, he needs purposeful activity in accordance with the injunction: "Whichever gift each of you have received, use it in service to one another, like good stewards dispensing the grace of God in its varied forms." From this, we may derive the three purposes of human work as follows:

First, to provide necessary and useful goods and services.

Second, to enable every one of us to use and thereby perfect our gifts like good stewards.

Third, to do so in service to, and in cooperation with, others, so as to liberate ourselves from our inborn egocentricity.

This threefold function makes work so central to human life that it is truly impossible to conceive of life at the human level without work. "Without work, all life goes rotten," said Albert Camus, "but when work is soulless, life stifles and dies."

→>-<-

Olive Pierce
Up River · 1996

It's a pity that it is not generally acknowledged that the value of a small proud community like the one on the Neck is inestimable. A quick look around the country and the world gives evidence that communities like it are dying out. The farmers and loggers of yesterday, if they haven't gone on to other occupations, are working minimum-wage jobs for giant companies or are living on welfare. But look at the merits of the way of life I have been documenting. The people have a tradition, a skill, a love of their work. They are self-sufficient, they take care of each other, they believe in family. They are not primarily consumers—they save and reuse. And their method of catching lobsters is not so mercilessly efficient that they ravage the ocean bottom as they make their catch.

If a national referendum were held, I would cast my vote for a culture that is rooted in the land and sea, where power resides in family and community and in wisdom passed from generation to generation.

→►◄←

Evan Eisenberg
The Ecology of Eden · 1998

Another, subtler effect becomes apparent when one hears our intellectuals talking about man, nature, and the future of the planet. "I am a child of the suburbs," one writes, "and even though I live on the edge of the wild I have only a tenuous understanding of the natural world. I can drive past hundreds of miles of fields without ever being able to figure out what's growing in them, unless it's corn." Although I now live among (dwindling) farms, and have written about agriculture, I guess I am only slightly better at this. I have done some gardening, but have never had to depend on it to keep me alive. How on earth are the likes of us going to act as poet-legislators for the planet, or as counselors in the marriage of man and nature? For all our tramping around in the woods, we are ecological celibates.

The contempt that many farmers, ranchers, loggers, and hunters feel for armchair environmentalists—even for active backpackers and birdwatchers—is not based solely in their wallets. In their heart of hearts, they feel that they know and even love nature better than the environmentalists do. In a sense, they are right. The backpacker loves nature chastely; the farmer wants to get a child upon her.

Just this, Wendell Berry would say, is the problem with modern nature-love, the love of Sierra Clubbers who look but don't touch. For we must touch nature somewhere, even if that somewhere is conveniently out of sight. And the more out of sight that somewhere is—the more removed from the gleaming nature of pinup calendars and television specials— the deeper the wound is likely to be.

-->-<-

The most interesting innovation the Malpai Group has devised is a program called the Grass Bank. "I was taught to manage for the bad times," Bill Miller told me as we watched the water in Sycamore Creek. "The good times take care of themselves." But sometimes, especially in this arid region, the bad times can't be managed, and a rancher is faced with selling some of his land to developers or selling his cattle, which is often equivalent to losing his ranch. This is not a range where cattle can be crowded. It takes 50 acres to support an animal unit (the equivalent of a mother cow and calf). Through the Grass Bank, the Malpai ranchers have essentially pooled their grass resources. When last year's drought hit his ranch, which he runs in partnership with his grandmother, Billy Darnell became one of the first to make use of the Grass Bank. He was allowed to graze his cattle on a section of the Gray Ranch that was unaffected by the drought. In return for access to the Grass Bank, he placed a conservation easement, held by the Malpai Group, upon his own ranch, which prevents it from being subdivided. In other words, the Grass Bank helps Darnell keep his ranch, and it assures his neighbors that the ranch will remain open and undeveloped—which is what Darnell wants in any case. "I was able to tell my banker, 'I'm resting my ranch,'" Darnell said, with an unfaded expression of surprise on his face.

So far, the cycle of the Grass Bank is not complete. Grass is worth money, and the rancher who lends his grass to a neighbor must be paid. The Gray Ranch, for instance, normally charges a grazing fee of $12 per animal unit per month. Several plans to raise money to recompense the Gray Ranch are in the works, but it's the Malpai Group, working as a whole, that is raising the money, not just Billy Darnell scrambling to keep his herd and, quite possibly, his ranch intact over the course of a single summer.

"What we discovered when we sat down and talked," Bill Miller told me as we walked along Sycamore Creek, "was that we had a lot of the same interests, a lot of the same long-term goals." The Glenns had told me the same thing, and they, like Miller, were referring not to discussions among the ranchers themselves but to discussions among ranchers, the Forest Service, the BLM, and, perhaps most surprisingly, The Nature Conservancy. In much of the American West, words like *environmentalist* and *the Feds* signal the end of meaningful debate, much as the word *cattle* does in some environmental circles. To some Nature Conservancy staffers, supporting cattle ranching made no sense, and to a few ranchers in the Malpai region, working with The Nature Conservancy or with federal agencies was simply anathema. But that is not how Bill Miller sees it. "Take the National Biological Service," he said, referring to a federal inventory of species that has aroused bitter controversy across the country and adverse congressional reaction. "I can use the results of that inventory as a management tool. It gives me greater knowledge of the habitat on my land." But he adds, "I flew over the Southwest for seven years for an oil company, inspecting pipeline. In all that time, I never once saw rangeland destroyed by cattle. By people, by bad grazing practices, yes. Never by cattle."

To a number of its most pressing concerns, notably a sense of isolation and helplessness, the Malpai Group has found workable answers. It has created what Bill McDonald calls a "radical center," a moderate, proactive response to the same problems of land use, property rights, and federal hegemony that seem to have inspired only extremism in many of its neighbors—including those in Catron County, New Mexico, just to the east, where it has been argued, in essence, that the federal government has no right to own property.

But the problems the Malpai ranchers face are not primarily political, they are economic. I don't mean the fact that cattle prices rise and fall or that some years are drier than others. I mean that these ranchers compete in a world where the measure of land is its productivity and where the only viable definition of productivity, so far, is a short-term one. "The land has got to be productive," I heard Warner Glenn, Bill Miller, and Ray Turner say at different times. By saying this, they aren't just articulating an old-fashioned Christian view about man's dominion over the creatures of the earth. They're arguing for what one neighbor calls "working wilderness." They're saying that unless there is some economic return from the land, there is no defense at all against the pressures of development, which are spiraling outward from nearly every city and small town in the West.

Some, of course, would argue that grazing 240 cattle on 15,000 acres of deeded and leased land, as the Glenns do, is not productive when you compare it with that land's value for housing developments of the kind that are proliferating in the Southwest. Some would argue that the most productive use of this biologically diverse region is ecotourism—forgetting, of course, that ecotourism is also a form of development, seldom benign. The real matter at stake in these borderlands is the fate of open land and the justification for it. In the West a small but growing movement claims that property rights are absolute, inviolable. The members of the Malpai Borderlands Group have decided for themselves that asserting absolute property rights will inevitably mean the destruction of the West, the disappearance of open land. They have found a series of shared possibilities, elective possibilities, that offer a potential that did not exist before, a potential they created among themselves. But to make use of those possibilities, there is a quid pro quo. You use the Grass Bank only by ceding development rights to the Malpai Group. You derive the benefits of neighboring only by contributing to the common good, not by vigilantly defending what you call your own.

It is a conceit in the West, often indulged, to allude to the pioneer ethic. You hear it in the suburbs of Denver, in Santa Fe, in Phoenix. It can be used to justify almost anything, from strip-mining to the Indian wars, from public politeness to an honest day's work. But what struck me in talking to the members of the Malpai Group—to the Glenns, to Bill McDonald, to Bill Miller and Billy Darnell, even to the Austins, who are relatively recent transplants from New York City—was the degree to which the interlacing of generations governed their thinking. In Bill Miller's voice you could hear his father's words, and in Billy Darnell's decision to make use of the Grass Bank you could hear his grandmother speaking, too. *And upon whom would you bestow the future except those who truly honor the past?*

You say that there are just two sides to this equation. There are the environmentalists—and the other side. I'm on the "other" side but not by my choice. I have worked my entire adult life striving to protect the earth's resources from being exploited. My time in the trenches is longer than I can remember, my scars are real, I will die engaged in the fight. I take pain at your insistence that because I do not choose to be a member of your "collective political party" (the environmental movement) that I am on the "other side." But it is not new experience for me to feel this way. Environmental organizations fight me, as a small organic farmer, rancher, tree-farmer, they fight me. They say I pollute the earth by applying manure to my field, while petroleum giants have succeeded in destroying the oceans. They say my cows pass gasses out of their lovely backends which damage the Ozone while US government stockpiles deadly nuclear waste and chemical weapons. They say I am immoral for selling my cattle to slaughter for meat. They say I subject my poor horses to involuntary servitude. They say my lands would be better for all of us as a wildlife preserve. This isn't about me or mine. I would suggest to you that there are many sides to the battle. There are environmental organizations, there are individuals, there is government, there is big business. In my humble opinion government and big business are chummy with the environmental organizations because they have seen the need for a political merger. And the vigilance of environmentalists needs a target, so the corporate attorneys and the federal granting agencies point out the little independent operators and say this is your villain. I'll work with you to keep the earth but don't call me an environmentalist. I'll not sign on to the collective. I'm an individual first, just like you. We can work together as a community if you wish.

-->-<-

"Let each individual do his daily chore of labor necessary to replace the goods and services which he consumes, and to provide support for the old, the sick and the children. Meanwhile, let him concentrate his chief energies on his major task of expression, unfoldment, improvement, creation."

—SCOTT NEARING, *The Making of a Radical*

-->-<-

JOHN STEINBECK
The Grapes of Wrath · 1938

When a horse stops working and goes into the barn there is a life and a vitality left, there is a breathing and a warmth, and the feet shift on the straw, and the jaws champ on the hay, and the ears and the eyes are alive. [. . .] But when the motor of a tractor stops, it is as dead as the ore it came from. The heat goes out of it like the living heat that leaves a corpse. Then the corrugated iron doors are closed and the tractor man drives home to town, perhaps twenty miles away, and he need not come back for weeks or months, for the tractor is dead. And this is easy and efficient. So easy that the wonder goes out of work, so efficient that the wonder goes out of land and the working of it, and with the wonder the deep understanding and the relation. And in the tractor man there grows the contempt that comes only to a stranger who has little understanding and no relation. For nitrates are not the land, nor phosphates; and the length of fibre in the cotton is not the land. Carbon is not a man, nor salt nor water nor calcium. He is all these, but he is much more, much more; and the land is so much more than its analysis. The man who is more than his chemistry, walking on the earth, turning his plough-point for a stone, dropping his handles to slide over an outcropping, kneeling in the earth to eat his lunch; that man who is more than his elements knows the land that is more than its analysis. But the machine man driving a dead tractor on land he does not know and love, understands only chemistry; and he is contemptuous of the land and of himself. When the corrugated iron doors are shut, he goes home and his home is not the land.

Chapter 7: Home

These readings suggest how conservation will become more relevant to Americans as we bring it home. Voltaire said, "We must all cultivate our garden" and make beautiful all that is close at hand. Wendell Berry shows how fundamental this is by reminding us that "you cannot know who you are until you know where you are." Honoring the familiar, the local, and the native is no ordinary thing, and becomes a path toward also honoring oneself and others. Conservation protects the rough edges in a world that is increasingly soft and similar and unspectacular. These edges, sometimes polished by human hands, are the nooks and crannies of a unique life. They are the natural places that inspire our thinking, replenish our souls, remind us that where we live is like no other place, and give us a hold in the world. There are, however, many legitimate reasons in this complex world why people benefit from starting over in a new place, and large-scale transience has become a hallmark of our culture.

What does it mean today to be at home in the world? How can land conservation offer the sense of responsibility and eagerness to engage with the land so that no one, no matter where they live, might ever feel homeless?

→>-<-

"This spot where you sit is your own spot. It is on this very spot and in this very moment that you can become enlightened. You don't have to sit beneath a special tree in a distant land."

—THICH NHAT HAHN

Like other Americans uncertain of who they are, I take a firm hold on the certainties of where I am from. I can say to myself that a good part of my private and social character, the kinds of scenery and weather and people and humor I respond to, the prejudices I wear like dishonorable scars, the affections that sometimes waken me from middle-aged sleep with a rush of undiminished love, the virtues I respect and the weaknesses I condemn, the code I try to live by, the special ways I fail at it and the kinds of shame I feel when I do, the models and heroes I follow, the colors and shapes that evoke my deepest pleasure, the way I adjudicate between personal desire and personal responsibility, have been in good part scored into me by that little womb-village and the lovely, lonely, exposed prairie of the homestead.

"Today, the open prairie is cobwebbed with paths that go from house to house . . . and each path is the line of an old friendship, a dependency, a working partnership. Imprinted with these ghostly social usages, the land, which looks so bare when one first sees it, ignorantly, from a car window, continues to have a people shape, a residual body of meaning of a kind that mere space cannot yield."

—JONATHAN RABHAN, *Bad Land*

SCOTT RUSSELL SANDERS
Staying Put · 1993

As a boy in Ohio, I knew a farm family, the Millers, who suffered from three tornadoes. The father, mother, and two sons were pulling into their driveway after church when the first tornado hoisted up their mobile home, spun it around, and carried it off. With the insurance money, they built a small frame house on the same spot.

Several years later, a second tornado peeled off the roof, splintered the garage, and rustled two cows. The Millers rebuilt again, raising a new garage on the old foundation and adding another story to the house. That upper floor was reduced to kindling by a third tornado, which also pulled out half the apple trees and slurped water from the stock pond. Soon after that I left Ohio, snatched away by college as forcefully as by any cyclone. Last thing I heard, the family was preparing to rebuild yet again.

Why did the Millers refuse to move? I knew them well enough to say they were neither stupid nor crazy. Plain stubbornness was a factor. These were people who, once settled, might have remained at the foot of a volcano or on the bank of a flood-prone river or beside an earthquake fault. They had relatives nearby, helpful neighbors, jobs and stores and schools within a short drive, and those were all good reasons to stay. But the main reason, I believe, was that the Millers had invested so much of their lives in the land, planting orchards and gardens, spreading manure on the fields, digging ponds, building sheds, seeding pastures. Out back of the house were groves of walnuts, hickories, and oaks, all started by hand from acorns and nuts. April through October, perennial flowers in the yard pumped out a fountain of blossoms. This farm was not just so many acres of dirt, easily exchanged for an equal amount elsewhere; it was a particular place, intimately known, worked on, dreamed over, cherished. [. . .]

The longing to become an inhabitant rather than a drifter sets me against the current of my culture, which nudges everyone into motion. Newton taught us that a body at rest tends to stay at rest, unless it is acted on by an outside force. We are acted on ceaselessly by outside forces—advertising, movies, magazines, speeches—and also by the inner force of biology. I am not immune to their pressure. Before settling in my present home, I lived in seven states and two countries, tugged from place to place in childhood by my father's work and in early adulthood by my own. This itinerant life is so common among the people I know that I have been slow to conceive of an alternative. Only by knocking against the golden calf of mobility, which looms so large and shines so brightly, have I come to realize that it is hollow. Like all idols, it distracts us from what is truly divine.

I am encouraged by the words of a Crow elder, quoted by Gary Snyder in *The Practice of the Wild:* "You know, I think if people stay somewhere long enough—even white people—the spirits will begin to speak to them. It's the power of the spirits coming up from the land. The spirits and the old powers aren't lost, they just need people to be around long enough and the spirits will begin to influence them."

As I write this, I hear the snarl of earth movers and chain saws a mile away destroying a farm to make way for another shopping strip. I would rather hear a tornado, whose damage can be undone. The elderly woman who owned the farm had it listed in the National Register, then willed it to her daughters on condition they preserve it. After her death, the daughters, who live out of state, had the will broken, so the land could be turned over to the chain saws and earth movers. The machines work around the clock. Their noise wakes me at midnight, at three in the morning, at dawn. The roaring abrades my dreams. The sound is a reminder that we are living in the midst of a holocaust. I do not use the word lightly. The earth is being pillaged, and every one of us, willingly or grudgingly, is taking part. We ask how sensible, educated, supposedly moral people could have tolerated slavery or the slaughter of Jews. Similar questions will be asked about us by our descendants, to whom we bequeath an impoverished planet. They will demand to know how we could have been party to such waste and ruin.

What does it mean to be alive in an era when the earth is being devoured, and in a country that has set the pattern for that devouring? What are we called to do? I think we are called to the work of healing, both inner and outer: healing of the mind through a change in consciousness, healing of the earth through a change in our lives. We can begin that work by learning how to inhabit a place.

"The man who is often thinking that it is better to be somewhere else than where he is excommunicates himself," we are cautioned by Thoreau, that notorious stay-at-home. The metaphor is religious: To withhold yourself from where you are is to be cut off from communion with the source. It has taken me half a lifetime of searching to realize that the likeliest path to the ultimate ground leads through my local ground. I mean the land itself, with its creeks and rivers, its weather, seasons, stone outcroppings, and all the plants and animals that share it. I cannot have a spiritual center without having a geographical one: I cannot live a grounded life without being grounded in a *place*.

In belonging to a landscape, one feels a rightness, an at-homeness, a knitting of self and world. This condition of clarity and focus, this being fully present, is akin to what the Buddhists call mindfulness, what Christian contemplatives refer to as recollection, what Quakers call centering down. I am suspicious of any philosophy that would separate this-worldly from other-worldly commitment. There is only one world, and we participate in it here and now, in our flesh and our place.

+>-<+

Jack Turner
The Abstract Wild · 1996

We know that the historical move from community to society proceeded by destroying local structures—religion, economy, food patterns, customs, possessions, families, traditions—and replacing these with national, or international, structures that created modern "individuals" and integrated them into society. Modern man lost his home; in the process everything else did, too. That is why Aldo Leopold's Land Ethic is so frighteningly radical; it renders this process *morally wrong*. "A thing is right when it tends to preserve the integrity, stability, and beauty of the biotic community. It is wrong when it tends otherwise." Apply this principle to people, animals, and plants, and the last ten thousand years of history is *evil*.

We are repeatedly told that the nature entertainment and recreation industries help the environment. After an orca killed another orca at Sea World, the veterinarian responsible for the whales claimed that children often "come away with knowledge they didn't have before and a fascination that doesn't go away . . . they become advocates for the marine environment." We hear the same general argument about national parks and wilderness areas; they must be entertaining and recreational or the public will not support environmental issues. And contact with exotic cultures is defended by saying it is required to save them.

This argument is no different from the one given by the Marine officer in Vietnam who explained the destruction of a village by saying, "We had to destroy it in order to save it." The first "it" here is real—people, plants, animals, houses: what was destroyed. The second "it" is abstract—a political category: the now nonexistent village we "saved" from the Viet Cong.

What, *exactly,* is the "it" we are trying to save in all the national parks, wilderness areas, sanctuaries, and zoos? What are we traveling abroad to find? I suggest that part of the answer is this: something connected with *our home*.

→><←

Harry S Truman
The Center of the World · *1957*

[*Editor's note:* The following transcript aired on National Public Radio's Lost and Found Sound Series. It was recorded in 1957, in President Harry S Truman's hometown of Independence, Missouri. Truman had been out of office for five years, and he'd been asked to speak at the groundbreaking ceremony for a new shopping center. He did, and he ended up improvising a bit. It's an elegy by a famous man for his boyhood home.]

Mr. Jim Burkes: (From vintage recording) And a very pleasant good morning to all of you to there. This is Jim Burkes speaking from the Truman Corners Town and Country Shoppers City, located at the intersection of Highway 71 and Blue Ridge Boulevard, approximately one mile northeast of Grandview and five and a half miles south of the southern limits of Kansas City, Missouri.

President Harry S Truman: It's a pleasure, indeed, to be present on an occasion like this. It gives a family rather a case of homesickness. This farm has been in the family nearly 100 years. It was bought by my grandfather back in the '60s. And it's home to all of us. We never spoke of any other place in the United States except this place right here as home.

My brother and sister and I were raised here. My sister was born here. My brother and I were not. We came here very shortly, though, before we were able to walk and talk and made a home here for our very younger days and then we've been here on this farm since 1905, as a home residence. My brother and I have planted and plowed corn and wheat and oats all over this acreage here.

It is now being turned into this wonderful business center. We sincerely hope that it'll be a profitable and successful one, because while we would like very much to have kept the farm as home and have used it and run it as a farm, we know very well that progress pays no attention to individuals. We don't want to stand in the way of progess, but that still doesn't keep us from being rather homesick for the places we knew of when we were children, places when we were three and five and two years old.

And it makes a great difference to all of you when a situation of that kind develops to the point where you can't even recognize where you are. I had to be told where to go when I came out here. I know every foot of this land and what's been growing on it and why it was here. There used to be a walnut grove right south of here. There was a great maple grove out in front. All this was prairie. It was first broken out and planted with a bull tongue. If some of you youngsters don't know what a bull tongue, you can get your dictionary and find out. It's north 80 here, made 125 bushels of corn to the acre by being dropped by hand. It was prairie sod and the people who were in the timber grows were absolutely certain that prairie land wasn't worth a hoot for anything. After these farms were broken out out here, all of them wished they had a part of them.

It's a very great pleasure indeed for me to have been able to fly back here from New York last night in order to be present for the dedication of this place. I am very fond of this location, always will be as long as I live. And when I get the false teeth and the cane and get bent over, you'll hear me pounding on the floor and telling the kids what a wonderful place this was before these birds ruined it.

Very happy indeed to have a part in this. I hope you'll all enjoy yourselves, and what's more than that, I hope you come out here and spend your money when the time comes, although we don't have a dime's worth of interest in what you do. But I hope every single one of you makes a grand success for coming to this business section. I know you'll like the place. It's the finest place in the world. And to me, it's the center of the world. And I've been around a great many places, but I never wanted to live anyplace but in Jackson County, Missouri, the finest county in the world.

"The officials thought it was a cruel joke to leave us stranded in the desert with no way to get home. What they didn't realize was that we were home, soul-centered and strong, women who recognized the sweet smell of sage as fuel for our spirits."

—TERRY TEMPEST WILLIAMS, *Refuge*

EVAN EISENBERG
The Ecology of Eden · *1998*

The one question the resident of a deluxe suburb (or of any Arcadia) must never ask himself is: What if everyone lived this way? In fact, this is a question that no resident of any

American-style suburb must ever ask himself. But though it has not been asked, the question is now being answered. Nearly half of all Americans live in suburbs. If most of those suburbs are far from deluxe, they still manage to use resources and generate waste at a rate never before achieved by large numbers of people anywhere on earth. A good measure of this is carbon emissions: the average American exhales (directly or indirectly) over five tons of carbon a year, or roughly five times the world average. While this figure is in part a mirror of wealth, it also reflects the peculiar facts of the suburban lifestyle. A single-family house that stands alone, naked to the elements, needs a great deal of energy for heating and cooling. (A row house uses 30 percent less, an apartment 40 percent less. In general, for each doubling of density in a metropolitan area, energy efficiency increases 30 percent.) No one can go anywhere except in a car. And since both the wildness of nature and the wildness of the city are far away, the main form of adventure is consumption.

"Home means staying put—staying put with life, with death, with the cold and the heat, with living next to neighbors who may be your relatives and also your enemies. It means reliving your history every time you walk the land because that history is written in the land. Home means building the present upon the landscape of the past."

—ANN FORBES, *The Boundary Keepers*

JAMES HOWARD KUNSTLER
The Geography of Nowhere · *1993*

Here is the quintessential New England town of America's fevered imagination in all its fine-boned details: the village green bordered by streets of white clapboard houses, stolid churches, and a handsome red-brick inn; the charming little commercial district with well-kept shops and cozy restaurants; the dignified old civic buildings unsullied by the affronts of Modernism; the brook that burbles through the heart of the village crossed by several quaint iron-railed bridges; the whole community of buildings wedged into a narrow valley between abrupt wooded hills so as to afford a pleasing sense of compactness and enclosure.

On a crisp October afternoon the scene was rich with paradoxes for a student of human ecology. Here were the week-ending corporate warriors, plying the sidewalks with their burnished wives, hunting for hand-crafted totem objects of hearth and home: the country quilts, the $38 carved birchwood salad forks, the whimsical pieces of "folk art" made twenty minutes ago. You knew these people were high-fliers because they stepped out of immaculate four-wheel-drive Jeeps, or else sedans of German manufacture, and they dressed in a kind of uniform: mint-condition expeditionary togs that had never been exposed to so much as a raindrop. The bull-like, middle-aged men also wore a slightly embarrassed, bewildered, and furtively resentful look on their faces, as though harboring deep doubts that shopping for handmade knickknacks was a virile pastime. And yet this is what their culture had reduced them to in their hours of leisure. They seemed especially dole-ful late in the day as they dutifully toted around the little twine-handled shopping bags that contained their wives' ceremonial purchases.

One sensed they saw in Woodstock some assemblage of symbols that spoke to them of a more spiritually gratifying way of life than the one they lived back home in the CEO enclaves of suburbia. I would even presume to summarize what it all signified to them: the idea of a true community organized at the human scale, along with a feeling of secure remoteness from the so-called modern world and all its terrors of gigantism and discontinuity. In short, Woodstock was more like home ought to be than their own homes were. As a legiti-mate yearning for a more humane living arrangement, this went beyond nostalgia—but it tended to express itself in senti-mental terms.

For instance, there were quite a few art galleries in Wood-stock filled with paintings that in one way or another tried to depict small town and rural life. Some of the paintings were very accomplished; some were amateurish. Some obviously tried to capture a contemporary scene (often of rural desola-tion) in a contemporary way; others blatantly resorted to clichés (covered bridges in the snow, et cetera). But they all had this in common: not one included an image of a car.

I asked the gallery owners what this signified and got a set of explanations ranging from "Beats me," to "Paintings with cars don't sell." Yet the village of Woodstock was jam-packed with cars, cars not just of great monetary value, but of great symbolic value to their owners—Mercedes Benzes, BMWs,

Land Rovers. The rural landscape around Woodstock was infested with cars. Every half-million-dollar vacation home, ancient or modern, had three or four parked in the driveway as did the few working farms that remained in the area. It was much easier to spot a car in Vermont than a cow.

Of course, the paintings were totem objects, invested with a specific set of symbolic meanings, in this case relating to the sense of place that is a part of every person's emotional equipment. People bought the paintings in order to bring a little sense of place home with them—home being somehow deficient in this quality.

All this is probably more or less obvious. But what is less obvious is the confusion that Americans feel about the entire issue of *place* and the abstract quality of their thinking about it. Hence the sentimentality. Everywhere in America, cars had destroyed the physical relationships between things and thereby destroyed the places themselves, and yet Americans could not conceive of life without cars. They couldn't imagine any modifications in their living arrangements that would make their home places more humane—for example, changing their zoning laws. They didn't want to challenge the status quo, or their own ideas about it. Undoubtedly, many of these visitors to Woodstock made money in the very enterprises that ruined places—like shopping plazas, or mass retailing, or any number of other endeavors that had the final consequence of making America ugly and killing local economies. This left them in quite a psychological pickle. What they did in the world and what they yearned for were at odds with each other. Unwilling to think clearly about the meaning of place in their lives, or their responsibility for making good places, they sought comfort in paintings of places with the cars deliberately left out. They finally reduced the whole question to just another commodity for consumption—shopping being one thing they could understand. This made them ridiculous and perhaps a little evil.

Unfortunately, what they yearn for—a place that feels like home ought to feel—is in short supply these days, and it can't really be bought, anyway. If it could be packaged and sold to individuals, then all the corporate warriors would live in better places than the jive-plastic residential enclaves where they return each night to watch TV, after a day's work in some distant elsewhere. But a community is something different from a commodity.

→><←

ANNIE DILLARD
Teaching a Stone to Talk · 1983

I alternate between thinking of the planet as home—dear and familiar stone hearth and garden—and as a hard land of exile in which we are all sojourners. Today I favor the latter view. The word "sojourner" occurs often in the English Old Testament. It invokes a nomadic people's sense of vagrancy, a praying people's knowledge of estrangement, a thinking people's intuition of sharp loss: "For we are strangers before thee, and sojourners, as were all our fathers: our days on the earth are as a shadow, and there is none abiding."

We don't know where we belong, but in times of sorrow it doesn't seem to be here, here with these silly pansies and witless mountains, here with sponges and hard-eyed birds. In times of sorrow the innocence of the other creatures—from whom and with whom we evolved—seems a mockery. Their ways are not our ways. We seem set among them as among lifelike props for a tragedy—or a broad lampoon—on a thrust rock stage.

It doesn't seem to be here that we belong, here where space is curved, the earth is round, we're all going to die, and it seems as wise to stay in bed as budge. It is strange here, not quite warm enough, or too warm, too leafy, or inedible, or windy, or dead. It is not, frankly, the sort of home for people one would have thought of—although I lack the fancy to imagine another.

The planet itself is a sojourner in airless space, a wet ball flung across nowhere. The few objects in the universe scatter. The coherence of matter dwindles and crumbles toward stillness. I have read, and repeated, that our solar system as a whole is careering through space toward a point east of Hercules. Now I wonder: what could that possibly mean, east of Hercules? Isn't space curved? When we get "there," how will our course change, and why? Will we slide down the universe's inside arc like mud slung at a wall? Or what sort of welcoming shore is this east of Hercules? Surely we don't anchor there, and disembark, and sweep into dinner with our host. Does someone cry, "Last stop, last stop"? At any rate, east of Hercules, like east of Eden, isn't a place to call home. It is a course without direction; it is "out." And we are cast.

These are enervating thoughts, the thoughts of despair. They crowd back, unbidden, when human life as it unrolls goes ill, when we lose control of our lives or the illusion of control, and it seems that we are not moving toward any end but merely blown. Our life seems cursed to be a wiggle merely, and a wandering without end. Even nature is hostile and poisonous, as though it were impossible for our vulnerability to survive on these acrid stones.

Whether these thoughts are true or not I find less interesting than the possibilities for beauty they may hold. We are down here in time, where beauty grows. Even if things are as bad as they could possibly be, and as meaningless, then matters of truth are themselves indifferent; we may as well please our sensibilities and, with as much spirit as we can muster, go out with a buck and wing.

The planet is less like an enclosed spaceship—spaceship earth—than it is like an exposed mangrove island beautiful and loose. We the people started small and have since accumulated a great and solacing muck of soil, of human culture. We are rooted in it; we are bearing it with us across nowhere. The word "nowhere" is our cue: the consort of musicians strikes up, and we in the chorus stir and move and start twirling our hats. A mangrove island turns drift to dance. It creates its own soil as it goes, rocking over the salt sea at random, rocking day and night and round the sun, rocking round the sun and out toward east of Hercules.

→>·<·⊷

ROBERT MICHAEL PYLE
The Thunder Tree · *1993*

Our concern for the absolute extinction of species is highly appropriate. As our partners in earth's enterprise drop out, we find ourselves lonelier, less sure of our ability to hold together the tattered business of life. Every effort to prevent further losses is worthwhile, no matter how disruptive, for diversity is its own reward. But outright extinction is not the only problem. By concentrating on the truly rare and endangered plants and animals, conservationists often neglect another form of loss that can have striking consequences: the local extinction. [. . .]

The third consequence amounts to a different kind of depletion. I call it the *extinction of experience*. Simply stated, the loss of neighborhood species endangers our experience of nature. If a species becomes extinct within our own radius of reach (smaller for the very old, very young, disabled, and poor), it might as well be gone altogether, in one important sense. To those whose access suffers by it, local extinction has much the same result as global eradication.

Of course, we are all diminished by the extirpation of animals and plants wherever they occur. Many people take deep satisfaction in wilderness and wildlife they will never see. But direct, personal contact with other living things affects us in vital ways that vicarious experience can never replace.

I believe that one of the greatest causes of the ecological crisis is the state of personal alienation from nature in which many people live. We lack a widespread sense of intimacy with the living world. Natural history has never been more popular in some ways, yet few people organize their lives around nature, or even allow it to affect them profoundly. Our depth of contact is too often wanting. Two distinctive birds, by the ways in which they fish, furnish a model for what I mean.

Brown pelicans fish by slamming directly into the sea, great bills agape, making sure of solid contact with the resource they seek. Black skimmers, graceful ternlike birds with longer lower mandibles than upper, fly over the surface with just the lower halves of their bills in the water. They catch fish too, but avoid bodily immersion by merely skimming the surface.

In my view, most people who consider themselves nature lovers behave more like skimmers than pelicans. They buy the right outfits at L. L. Bean and Eddie Bauer, carry field guides, and take walks on nature trails, reading all the interpretive signs. They watch the nature programs on television, shop at the Nature Company, and pay their dues to the National Wildlife Federation or the National Audubon Society. These activities are admirable, but they do not ensure truly intimate contact with nature. Many such "naturalists" merely skim, reaping a shallow reward. Yet the great majority of the people associate with nature even less.

When the natural world becomes chiefly an entertainment or an obligation, it loses its ability to arouse our deeper instincts. Professor E. O. Wilson of Harvard University, who has won two Pulitzer prizes for his penetrating looks at both humans and insects, believes we all possess what he calls "bio-philia." To Wilson, this means that humans have an innate desire to connect with other life forms, and that to do so is highly salutary. Nature is therapeutic. As short-story writer Valerie Martin tells us in "The Consolation of Nature," only nature can restore a sense of safety in the end. But clearly, too few people ever realize their potential love of nature. So where does the courtship fail? How can we engage our biophilia?

Everyone has at least a chance of realizing a pleasurable and collegial wholeness with nature. But to get there, intimate association is necessary. A face-to-face encounter with a banana slug means much more than a Komodo dragon seen on television. With rhinos mating in the living room, who will care about the creatures next door? At least the skimmers are aware of nature. As for the others, whose lives hold little place for nature, how can they even care?

The extinction of experience is not just about losing the personal benefits of the natural high. It also implies a cycle of disaffection that can have disastrous consequences. As cities and metastasizing suburbs forsake their natural diversity, and their citizens grow more removed from personal contact with nature, awareness and appreciation retreat. This breeds apathy toward environmental concerns and, inevitably, further degradation of the common habitat.

So it goes, on and on, the extinction of experience sucking the life from the land, the intimacy from our connections. This is how the passing of otherwise common species from our immediate vicinities can be as significant as the total loss of rarities. People who care conserve; people who don't know don't care. What is the extinction of the condor to a child who has never known a wren?

→>—<+

Robert Coles
Children of Crisis · 1967

I am writing about the land. I am writing about people, of course, about fellow citizens, and particularly about children, who live uprooted lives, who have been stranded, who are hidden from the rest of us. Nevertheless, I am writing about the land, miles and miles of it, the rich American earth. I am also writing about *a* land, the United States of America, some country that is hilly and rocky and often windswept or fog-covered, some that is a plateau, high and leveled-off and dry, some that is low and flat and at the water's edge. More precisely, I suppose, I am trying to approach the lives of certain individuals who may in various ways differ, as members or representatives of this or that "group" of people, but who for all of that share something hard to define exactly or label with a few long and authoritative words, something that has to do with the way people, however unlike in appearance or background, manage to live on the land and come to terms with it, every day of their lives. [. . .]

Certainly it is true that migrant farm workers don't look upon their experiences the way casual travelers might. Nor do share-croppers wax lyrical about the South, that haunting, mysterious, strangely uncommon region which has both defied and invited descriptions all through American history. Mountaineers have their ballads to sing, their guitars to "pick" away at, but they don't stand on ridges or the edges of plateaus or way up on peaks in order to get breathtaking views, which are then photographed and thereby carried home, to be shown one evening after another. No, in Logan County, West Virginia, mountaineers don't find themselves quaint; and in Adams County, Mississippi, tenant farmers don't burble about those antebellum homes, or gush in pride and awe at the river, the great god of a river; and in Collier County, Florida, or Palm Beach County, Florida, migrant workers don't join hands with conservationists and worry about wildlife in the beautiful, ever spectacular Everglades. [. . .]

I have watched mountaineers slip through mountain passes and valleys toward Dayton, say, or Chicago—all too willingly, because work and the food money can buy is far better than constant and unappeased hunger. As they get ready to leave, those many men and women and children, they deny having any regrets. And yet they do: they are losing something; they feel low and sad; more precisely, they anticipate the yearning they may later have, the homesickness, the lovesickness, the sense of bereavement. Dispossessed, they have to leave; they ought to leave. It was an awful life. And yet—one more time: "If I don't have to go, maybe it'll be my sons. They'll be the ones to cry and not me. They'll be happy. I know. They'll be looking ahead, I know. But it'll be a shame for us to leave, my family; it's a shame when you leave the only thing you've known, your land—and remember, it's land that's seen you trying and that's tried back, tried to give you all it could. There's no land up there, just people and buildings. I know that. That's too bad. That's the way it has to be; I know it. I do.

But I don't have to like it. I don't. I never will, even if I have to
say good-bye and go on up the road myself, away from here,
from my land."

→>-<-

MARY OLIVER
Wild Geese · 1992

You do not have to be good.
You do not have to walk on your knees
for a hundred miles though the desert, repenting.
You only have to let the soft animal of your body love
    what it loves.
Tell me about despair, yours, and I will tell you mine.
Meanwhile the world goes on.
Meanwhile the sun and the clear pebbles of the rain
are moving across the landscapes,
over the prairies and the deep trees,
the mountains and the rivers.
Meanwhile the wild geese, high in the clean blue air,
are heading home again.
Whoever you are, no matter how lonely,
the world offers itself to your imagination,
calls to you like the wild geese, harsh and exciting—
over and over announcing your place
in the family of things.

→>-<-

"No people on earth has sprung from the soil of its place. Even the Aborigines are not aboriginal, but came to Australia within the last twenty thousand years. No culture is pure. All are products of history, of migrations, of hybridization."

—EVAN EISENBERG, *The Ecology of Eden*

+>-<+

RACHEL L. BAGBY
Daughter of Growing Things · 1990

[*Editor's note:* This is an interview between Rachel Bagby and her mother, a well-known urban gardener in Philadelphia.]

Daughter: Tell me a little about your background. *I* know it. *You* know it, but tell me again so I can get it on this tape.

Mother: See, what give me the idea to do this, is I just got sick and tired of walking by weeds. Absolutely a disgrace to me. Instead of growing weeds, if weeds can grow where there's nothing but cement and bricks and stuff, if weeds can grow in there, something else can grow also. And you have the weeds taller than I am. People be afraid to go by Twenty-first Street. That's where we had to go to go to the store, and people would snatch pocketbooks and run over you, and you couldn't find them in the weeds. So that's how we got started with that. Now, when I was home, I came up on the farm . . .

Daughter: Home where?

Mother: South Carolina. I came up on a farm. My father was a farmer. [. . .]

Daughter: How do you think what you do relates to ecology, relates to the Earth? How do you talk about that?

Mother: Well, I talk about it like I always do, 'cause this is where you see the real nature of the universe. The real one, without . . . before it's transformed into different things. Because even children don't have the least idea of the food they eat. What grows in the ground, what grows on top, what good for blood, what good for different things. A lot of adults don't have any idea. So that's how I relate it to everyday living.

You get firsthand . . . everybody get a firsthand look at real nature. That's how I see it. That's how I love it. You can see it come up, you can see it grow and you see how it grows, and see it die if you don't take care of it. That tells you something.

Daughter: What does it tell you?

Mother: It tells you that if you're not taken care of, tells you, you got to take care of whatever you have. If you don't it will die then, or grow wild like the things in the fields, out in the woods. God has created things to stay alive without being taken care of but you can't try to, like to say, try to tame them. If you try to tame them you have to give them some of that that they get ordinarily. But the Earth is created so that everything should be taken care of. [. . .]

Daughter: Do you work with children a lot in the garden?

Mother: I love to, yes. I generally have them in there and showing them the grass from the weeds and from the plants and how it looks and how they grow, too. The grass grows, too. The weeds grow, too. That's part of nature. They say, "What good are they?" This can be a fertilizer for next year.

"What!? Weeds!?" You let them sit there and rot and that replenish the Earth. See, everything has a cycle. See, those the kinda things.

Daughter: How do you get the children in there?

Mother: All you have to do is open the gate and say "Come on children." If I had more strength I'd have all the kids in there, but I don't have the strength anymore and I can't get anyone interested in the children. The mothers say, yeh, take the children so they can sit down and look at television. But all the kids that I have met want to get out there in the garden and they beg you to let them come in and help. It takes a lot of time with children. And I don't have that much time trying to do all these other things. But I would just have someone to just go with them. I don't have that. The mothers not interested anymore. "I gotta look at my soap opera." And they are their children. "Here, you can take 'em, I gotta look at my soap opera. I'll give you money. Take 'em to such and such a thing. You take 'em while I sit and watch my soap opera, or do anything else." So those opposition you get now.

Daughter: And what kind of hope do you have? Even with that opposition, how do you keep on going?

Mother: Faith. I know out of all of that, it may be one or two that you'll get through to. Even with one, I'll be thankful. You know. Faith. Just keep on going. You do that with children, all of them will not end up in jail. Some of 'em come out all right. But you don't look for a whole lot. You don't expect a whole lot.

Daughter: Why do you think that if you show them the living things that will help them straighten up?

Mother: It help, it helps them to . . . I think it will help them to appreciate the beauty of the Earth, and of nature; we call it mother nature.

Daughter: Do you think it helps them appreciate the beauty of each other and their abilities?

Mother: This is the thing. If you can appreciate the Earth, you can appreciate the beauty of yourself. Even if this has beauty, I, too, have beauty. The same creator created both. And if I learned to take care of that I'll also take care of myself and help take care of others. See, taking care of yourself and appreciating yourself is the first step. But you can't go with a child and say that. You know, you show 'em this and they'll say, "ummmm," you know, some of these other things'll come to them themselves, or "if this is it, then I, look at me." Then they won't feel so let down all the time. Sometime we fail in trying to do that.

Daughter: What do you mean you may fail?

Mother: Sometime you may fail, the children may not get it. They may not. Like I say, you may get one or two. That's what I mean. I am who I am whether I'm black, blue, or brown. I'm a human being. Therefore, I stand for just as much right as you stand for although my color is different, you see. I'm no less than you are regardless of my color.

Daughter: You see the children move past some of that as a result of working?

Mother: Yes. Yes. They compare sometimes so you let them see pictures of other children working, say, "Well, I can do it as well as he can do it."

Daughter: You show them pictures of other children working?

Mother: Right. And then see that's giving them confidence in themselves that they can do things, too, other than throw a ball and bat a ball. Other than break out people's windows and curse in the street. "If they can stop and make things, make a beautiful plant, so can I." Some of them will stop and say that. And they'll tell you, "Let's do our garden."

→>◄←

"There is only this solid sense of having had or having been or having lived something real and good and satisfying, and the knowledge that having had or been or lived these things I can never lose them again. Home is what you can take away with you."

—WALLACE STEGNER, *Marking the Sparrow's Fall*

Chapter 8: Storytelling

This chapter asks us to view storytelling not as an amenity, but as a fundamental tool in the creation of an enduring land ethic. It has been difficult for our movement to honor both the place and the idea, the how and the why, of land conservation, even though a land ethic demands both the vital place and the well-understood idea. Places can be protected through our laws and through our existing market systems. Ideas, however, can be protected only through the constant use of stories, metaphors, and symbols. Protecting the place gives us great hope while preserving the idea gives us enormous meaning. Our culture offers all kinds of stories, but those from the land enable us to talk and think about something beyond ourselves. Land conservation gives people the opportunity to begin to create their own native stories. Our willingness to tell stories about the land gives the land larger meaning in our lives. If mythology is a true story where the facts have been made up, then stories from the experience of land conservation can come to symbolize another way of living on this earth.

What are good land conservation stories? How might we place more of an emphasis on storytelling in our daily work?

→>◄←

ROBERT ARCHIBALD
The Places of Stories · 1995

Our propensity for words, language, and story is not learned. We are born with the capacity for speaking with words, for telling stories, for describing who we are, and for remembering.

Our narratives transcend fact, for they are formed from the delicious emotional nuances of sensation: sound, smell, moods, sensuality, taste, color, shadow, texture, rhythm, cadence, tears, laughter, warmth, and coolness all experienced here, at a place on this earth.

Place and story are inseparable. "No place" is transformed to "place" as we imbue it with story and imprint both story and place as a singularity upon our consciousness. By giving places a name and a story, I can contemplate and describe them and, in the most ancient sense, call them into existence. We create ourselves from stories that conjoin us to places; bind us to each other; blend individual and communal identities; and provide definition, context and continuity, perspective, and personality. These stories of ourselves are works in progress until death.

Unfortunately, parts of our world are "no places." We have truncated our stories, creating profound disorientation and dislocation. Without coherent stories, we are diminished, uncertain, isolated. Without stories, places are desolate.

John Bratkowski, like his parents, was born on St. Louis' Old North Side, where his grandparents settled when they arrived from Poland at the turn of the century. I met Bratkowski last August at Crown Candy Kitchen, a real ice cream parlor on the corner of 14th and St. Louis Avenue. "How is the neighborhood?" I asked Bratkowski. "Hanging on," he replied, "which is better than I can say for most of the north side of the city." He cannot imagine living anywhere but here because his stories are all intertwined with this place. Neither could his parents, who lived their lives here and were born just three blocks from each other. Before Bratkowski left for the evening, he proudly showed me a flyer for the annual celebration of the Polish Falcons and urged me to come.

Crown Candy bustled with patrons on that Wednesday evening. This is how it has been since 1913, when the soda fountain opened in this then-vibrant neighborhood. Bratkowski may think this neighborhood is hanging on, but he is an optimist. Burned hulks of rowhouses, boarded-up corner stores, the one Catholic Church that still offers mass in Polish, and even the delicious bounty of Crown Candy Kitchen are reminders of now-dissipated community life, buttressed by the ominous dearth of people on the streets. Neighbors rarely congregate the way they once did. Although the Polish Falcons forlornly hang on to a century-long tradition in this place, the stories of this place are disappearing.

With their decline, the neighborhood too is diminishing, both physically and in the minds of the residents. The remembrances that once made this neighborhood a place with stories that linked people to each other has somehow reversed its course, receding into a forgetfulness that buries the place in oblivion.

Yet there is a shadow here of a place that once worked. This community was built at a time when most people did not have cars, when, in neighborhood streets, all of life's necessities could be found—supplies of all kinds, purchased over the counter from clerks and merchants who were also friends, relatives, and neighbors. People mingled on the streets, in the shops and taverns, in the beauty parlors and barbershops, at wakes and weddings and school carnivals. Children congregated in the same places as the adults, hearing and learning the stories. Idle hours were full of conversations with neighbors, sometimes in the social clubs and cafes and bars, but also over back fences, on the steps of the church, at the gate of the schoolyard, on the walk to the bakery and the butcher shop.

Neighbors created their stories and their place. They discussed who needed help because of illness or bad luck; or who had beaten his wife and who should tell the priest; who was letting his house rundown or whose children were misbehaving; how soon the alderman would see to those street repairs and which team would win the baseball game tomorrow afternoon at Sportsman's Park. In this way, they defined their values, enforced standards of conduct, and looked out for each other. They escaped isolation and found life in stable relationships with each other.

The neighborhood itself was a singular concoction of place consisting of webbed relationships between its people and stories of times past that explained who they were and what was so special about their place. There were few sharp dividing lines, but rather a seamless, storied whole, bound together by shared experience that gave form, meaning, and embellishment to life.

Now the windows at Crown Candy Kitchen are closed even in summer, the once-essential ceiling fans merely stirring the chilled air that comes from the machine in the front corner. "How many of the people in here are from the neighborhood?" I ask. Bratkowski looks around at the fifty or so people in the shop. "I count three or four," he says. These people come here from other parts of the city, even from the suburbs just to revel in good ice cream, decadent sauces, and nostalgia. They come looking for life the way it used to be, but the people and the stories are gone, and with them have gone the sense of place these non-neighbors seek. No new stories will be told tonight, for the people are only customers and the stories once told in these booths have been necessarily replaced with transactions, albeit tasty ones. This is not their place; the customers do not know who lives around the corner or on the next block, and they do not know each other. They do not go to church or school together, and they certainly do not walk home together. And they do not have stories in common.

For fifty years, the people who made this a place have been getting in their cars and leaving, making the community obsolete. Between 1950 and 1990, the St. Louis region's population increased 133 percent; but the amount of developed land increased by 355 percent. The people who live here have simply moved farther apart. This has happened everywhere in our nation, not just in old cities. It has happened in my hometown on Michigan's Upper Peninsula. It has happened in Salina, Kansas, and to the few hundred people of Brown's Valley, Minnesota. Some of the postwar boom cities were built this way intentionally; Albuquerque, Los Angeles, Phoenix, Dallas, and Houston, to name just five. Changes in federal housing policy at war's end made it cheaper to buy a new house in the suburbs than to stay in older neighborhoods, and interstate highways made it quick and easy to traverse back and forth to work. The suburbs were seductively different but, as many discovered, a Faustian bargain, for the suburbs were a "no place."

More than half of all Americans, including me, now live in such places. I live in a relatively affluent suburb of St. Louis.

What we have in common are similar incomes and material standards of living. Real estate values are a paramount concern and the most frequent topic of conversation. The subdivision is governed by covenants, a privatized form of government instituted to protect real estate values and ensure uniformity. Clothes lines and birdhouses are not allowed. Cars may not be regularly parked on the streets, boats may not be kept in driveways, children's toys and bicycles may not be left outside, and no outbuildings may be erected. Each house has at least a two-car garage set back at a uniform distance from the street, and all have central air-conditioners. As families become even more affluent or suffer financial reverses, or when the children leave for college, the For Sale signs go up.

People really do not live in this subdivision; they just sleep, watch television, and sometimes eat here. We do not share anything except proximity, income levels, and real estate values. There are no common stories here, no common concerns, no civic life, no sets of reciprocal obligations except those listed in the real estate covenants. It is not a real "place," because it has no history and no lives are lived and shared here. This is the story of decline of community life in the second half of the twentieth century. No matter where we live, it is now our story.

You cannot exist in this subdivision without an automobile. It is too far to walk to work or to school or to church, to the park, the grocery store, the barbershop, the nearest restaurant, the library. And so our communities have become environmentally hazardous. The attributes that have rendered them storyless have also made them prodigious consumers of energy —automobile dependency, increased commuting distances, increased gasoline consumption, central air conditioning, destruction of agricultural land, increased water runoff, prodigious demand for highway construction, and pressure on all other vital infrastructure.

Yet not just suburbs, but even intact urban neighborhoods and small towns have lost the characteristics that made Old North St. Louis a community—shared lives, shared space, and a public or civic life in which all accepted mutual obligations for the welfare of the whole. We cannot solve these problems on a grand national scale. What is possible is for us to rethink our own lives, to resurrect and reconstruct communities rooted in place and based on relationships, where we learn to redefine happiness based on the quality of our relationships with our place and with our people, not on our ability to consume. If we can do these things, not only can we be happier, but we will tread more lightly, consume less, pollute less, recycle more. This, of course, is not only a recipe for happier people and functional communities, but it is also a prescription for a healthier planet.

→>◄←

GARY PAUL NABHAN
Cultures of Habitat · 1997

To restore any place, we must also begin to re-story it, to make it the lesson of our legends, festivals, and seasonal rites. Story is the way we encode deep-seated values within our culture. Ritual is the way we enact them. We must ritually plant the cottonwood and willow poles in winter in order to share the sounds of the vermilion flycatcher during the rites of spring. By replenishing the land with our stories, we let the wild voices around us guide the restoration work we do. The stories will outlast us. When such voices are firmly rooted, the floods of modern technological change—of border-blasting radios and all-night pornography shows—won't ever have a chance to dislodge them from this earth.

→>─<←

"Writing and reading decrease our sense of isolation. They deepen and widen and expand our sense of life: they feed the soul. When writers make us shake our heads with the exactness of their prose and their truths, and even make us laugh about ourselves or life, our buoyancy is restored. We are given a shot at dancing with, or at least clapping along with, the absurdity of life, instead of being squashed by it over and over again. It's like singing on a boat during a terrible storm at sea. You can't stop the raging storm, but singing can change the hearts and spirits of the people who are together on that ship."

—ANNE LAMOTT, *Bird by Bird*

→>─<←

EDDY L. HARRIS
Solo Faces · 1997

In 1985, when I was 30 years old and living in St. Louis, I decided to canoe the Mississippi River from its source in Minnesota down to New Orleans and write a book about the trip. It was an impetuous plan, and one for which I was quite ill-prepared.

I'd scarcely been in a canoe before. I'd been camping perhaps twice in my entire life.

Growing up in St. Louis, the closest I came to the outdoors was the time or two I walked in the Missouri woods, clutching a shotgun in my hands, with my oldest brother at my side. He was a hunter and a fisherman, but his hunting and fishing were of the straightforward putting-meat-on-the-table variety. No fancy gear, no exotic locales, and the trophies were ducks from the lake, rabbits from the woods, catfish from the river.

My father would sometimes accompany us. I had noticed that he would never venture into the woods alone without carrying a gun, and he discouraged me from ever heading out into the countryside by myself. When I was in the Boy Scouts, he refused to let me go camping. His justification was always the same: snakes. "What do you want to sleep out in the woods for?" he'd say. "You want to get bit by a copperhead?"

If you're not accustomed to it, of course, the deep woods can be a frightening place, with its twigs snapping in the night, its snakes and bears and mountain lions that know no discrimination based on color or race. But I always suspected there was something else that my dad was afraid of. The other boys in my all-black Scout troop rarely went camping either. I sensed that their parents might have had the same fears.

Yet in the fall of 1985 I cast aside all that dread and canoed the length of the Mississippi River. Somewhere in the cane-brake of Tennessee, I set up camp in the midst of a downpour. It rained all night long and well into the morning. At some point a pack of wild animals wandered up in the dark and snuggled around the edges of my tent to steal a bit of my warmth.

When I poked on the bulges in the tent wall, they growled at me—feral dogs. They had me pinned down and so terrified that I could not sleep. I lay packed tight in my bedroll and clutched the pistol I'd brought along. When I finally bolted from the tent the next morning, one of the dogs chased me. I aimed the pistol at his chest and fired a single shot. The rest of the pack fled back into the woods.

But later still during that same voyage, on another night, at another campsite, a different source of fear came creeping out of the woods toward me. Nearing my trip's end, I made my camp on the Mississippi side of the river. I pitched my tent, built a fire, and started cooking my dinner. A possum rustled the leaves. When the branches rustled a second time, I thought nothing of it.

Then out of the woods came the bad dream. On the edge of the darkness, where the light from my campfire faded into shadows, stood the figures that must haunt the imagination of every black American who has heard the old stories about Emmer Till and James Earl Chaney and Willie Edwards. Two greasy-haired, camo-wearing white hunters materialized out of the forest lining the river and aimed their shotguns at me.

"Hey," one of them said. "Look what we got here."

"And I haven't shot at anything all day," the other one said.

It was deer season and they'd been out hunting, without success. I was not about to be used for target practice in the night. So I pulled the pistol from my boot and I shot in their general direction. When they scattered, I hastily broke camp and, wrought up with anger and fear, hopped into my canoe and sprinted for the middle of the river.

As I paddled toward the Gulf of Mexico, I was certain of the malevolence of man, and of those two men in particular. But as I reflect upon it now, it occurs to me that there might not have been anything particularly racial about that situation. And I suppose it's possible, remotely possible, that I reacted prematurely, an impulsive response rooted in the old black-and-white fears that I had hauled downriver with me. Perhaps.

The natural world, however, is neither black nor white. It is forest green, desert ocher, deep ocean blue. If there are barriers that keep us all from immersing ourselves in it and savoring its riches, they may be reducible, in part, to economics, to geography, to history, and to culture. But mostly they exist in our minds, in the fears and misperceptions that continue to keep us suspended in our separate limbos, unable to come together, even in a place as universally inviting as the world outside our doors.

"And when the story ended, we could also feel the absence of that rightness—the rightness of shared experience in the world around us, where experience has become solitary, fragmented. Pak Tua often talked about that disjuncture between the shared experience of the story and the solitary, unshareable experience of living in a world where there is nothing to listen to anymore, and nothing to tell, a world where the *turi-turin*, the oral tradition, is a nostalgic interlude rather than a pattern picked from the fabric of daily life."

—MARY STEEDLY, *Hanging Without a Rope*

"Because we use them to motivate and explain our actions, the stories we tell change the way we act in the world."

—WILLIAM CRONON, *A Place for Stories*

→>•<←

BARRY LOPEZ
Crow and Weasel · 1990

Half the cycle of the moon found them past the lake country, back on a path that bore their tracks. They rode for some days toward the forest. One evening before they stopped to camp they were hailed by someone in the fading light. They saw it was Badger when they rode up. She bid them enter her lodge, which was underground.

"I heard you coming toward me all day," said Badger with pleasure and excitement. "I hear everything, through the ground. Where have you come from?"

"We have been far to the north, but we live far away to the south and are headed home," said Crow.

"Well, you must stay here the night, and tell me of where you have been. There is good grass here for your horses, and no one around to bother them. We will have a good dinner and you will leave refreshed in the morning."

Crow and Weasel had never seen a lodge quite like Badger's. Quivers and parfleches, all beautifully decorated, hung from the walls, along with painted robes, birdbone breastplates, and many pieces of quillwork—leggings and moccasins, elktooth dresses, awl cases, and pipe bags. Lances decorated with strips of fur and small colored stones stood in the corners, and painted shields were hung on the walls beside medicine bundles. Other bundles were suspended from tripods.

Badger made up a good meal, and after they ate, Crow offered the pipe. In the silence that followed, Crow and Weasel felt a strange obligation to speak of what they had seen.

"Now tell me, my friends, what did you see up north? I have always wanted to know what it is like up there."

Weasel began to speak.

"My friend," said Badger. "Stand up, stand up here so you can express more fully what you have seen."

Weasel stood up, though he felt somewhat self-conscious in doing so. He began to speak about the people called Inuit and their habit of hunting an unusual white bear.

"Wait, my friend," said Badger. "Where were you when this happened?"

"We were in their camp. They told us."

"Well, tell me something about their camp."

Weasel described their camp, and then returned again to the story of hunting the bear.

"But, my friend," interrupted Badger, "tell me a little first of who these people are. What did they look like?"

Badger's words were beginning to annoy Weasel, but Crow could see what Badger was doing, and he smiled to himself. Weasel began again, but each time he would get only a little way in his story before Badger would ask for some point of clarification. Weasel was getting very irritated.

Finally Crow spoke up.

"Badger," he said, "my friend is trying very hard to tell his story. And I can see that you are only trying to help him, by teaching him to put the parts together in a good pattern, to speak with a pleasing rhythm, and to call on all the details of memory. But let us now see if he gets your meaning, for my friend is very smart."

"That is well put," said Badger, curious.

"Weasel," continued Crow, "do you remember what that man said before he began to tell us stories about Sedna and those other beings? He said, 'I have put my poem in order on the threshold of my tongue.' That's what this person Badger, who has taken us into her lodge, is saying. Pretend Badger and I are the people waiting back in our village. Speak to us with that kind of care."

Badger looked at Crow with admiration. Weasel, who had been standing uneasily before them, found his footing and his voice. He began to speak with a measured, fetching rhythm, painting a picture of the countryside where they had been, and then drawing the Inuit people and the others, the caribou, up into life, drawing them up out of the ground.

When Weasel finished, Badger nodded with gratitude, as though she had heard something profound.

"You know," she said to Weasel, "I have heard wondrous rumors of these Inuit people, but you are the first person I've heard tell a story about them who had himself been among them. You make me marvel at the strangeness of the world. That strangeness, the intriguing life of another people, it is a crucial thing, I think, to know."

"Now Crow," said Weasel, taking his seat, "tell Badger of our people and of our village. Tell her about this journey of ours."

Crow took his place in front of the other two. He also felt awkward, but with the help of Badger, a few pointed questions to sharpen his delivery, he began to speak strongly, with deliberation and care, about all that Weasel had asked him to say.

"You are fine young men," said Badger when Crow had finished. "I can see that. But you are beginning to sense your responsibilities, too, and the journey you have chosen is a hard one. If you keep going, one day you will be men. You will have families."

"We are very grateful for your hospitality, Badger," said Crow. "Each place we go, we learn something, and your wisdom here has helped us."

"I would ask you to remember only this one thing," said Badger. "The stories people tell have a way of taking care of them. If stories come to you, care for them. And learn to give them away where they are needed. Sometimes a person needs a story more than food to stay alive. That is why we put these stories in each other's memory. This is how people care for themselves. One day you will be good storytellers. Never forget these obligations."

No one since Mountain Lion had spoken so directly to them of their obligations, but this time Crow and Weasel were not made uncomfortable. Each could understand what Badger was talking about, and each one knew that if his life went on he would one day know fully what Badger meant. For now, all it meant was that it was good to remember and to say well what happened, if someone asked to hear.

In the morning when they left, Badger told them a way to get through the forest that was not quite so difficult as the way they had come. "It is an open trail," she said, "and there are not so many trees. You will be able to go more quickly. But, still, it is a long way to your country. And soon it will be the first Snow Moon."

She gave them each a winter robe of buffalo. They gave her a beaded bag from home, which she accepted with wonder and humility. And they said goodbye.

→>—<←

Ann Forbes
Thin Places · 1995

Each morning we awoke in the dark. We walked all day along steep narrow trails, fording icy streams overflowing from the monsoon rains, and climbing from five thousand feet in Hedangna over two sixteen-thousand-foot passes and up the Barun Valley. In five days, we covered the same distance I had covered in two weeks the previous spring while trekking with family. The villagers would stop only at dusk, when we had reached a cave large enough to hold all twenty-five of us. We ate one meal of rice a day, mixed with wild plants gathered along the trail. While hiking we snacked on roasted corn flour. Occasionally, we drank black tea.

By the third afternoon, we arrived at Yangle Meadow, the grazing lands at thirteen thousand feet below the Khembalung caves. We sat on the grassy floor of the narrow valley, flanked on either side by towering granite cliffs. Our words were swallowed by the roar of the Barun River, which carved its way through the center of the valley. Jadu Prasad pointed out some invisible trail going straight up the vertical rock face: the path to the caves. I sat silently. A chill that had been with me the entire trip slowly crept up from my stomach. The two oldest women in the group, both in their seventies, looked at the cliff and then looked at me. "Don't go," they said. "Don't do it. The trail is too hard. Stay below and wait."

I know how to rock climb, I know what to be afraid of, and I shared their concern. "If these grandmothers can do it, of course you can," Jadu Prasad said. Having spent much of the past year trying to keep up with these same grandmothers while collecting firewood and stinging nettle in the jungles around Hedangna, I wasn't so sure. But the men promised we would all go together the next morning and that they would look out for me. If I could go with them, I agreed, I would give it a try. We lifted our loads and went in search of a dry cave for the night.

The next morning we again awoke in the dark. It was drizzling. It had rained all night, and I had slept fitfully, dreaming of slippery mud and slippery rocks. I again asked Jadu Prasad if he thought I could make it and he again reassured me, so I went with the women to bathe. The women were used to doing things on their own; they were strong, and they assumed I was equally strong. I couldn't count on them for help on the trail. After a perfunctory bath in the icy water, I returned to an empty cave. I waited, thinking the men must have gone to bathe as well.

Finally, one man returned. He was surprised to see me, said the men had already left, and that he had just come back to get something he had forgotten. I grabbed my bag and scrambled after him. We walked silently and rapidly through the drizzle, turning off the main trail onto a narrow overgrown path that climbed toward the cliff. We caught up with Jadu Prasad and the two Brahmans. They greeted us as we approached and told me that the trail was too slippery for my boots, that I should go barefoot; they then returned to their discussion of whether the two menstruating women should climb to the sacred caves. I was curious to hear what they had to say, but was distracted by the trail and, now, by my bare feet. I had always imagined the pain the rocks and roots must bring to their feet. Until now I had never thought of the cold. The soles of my feet were numb, so numb I didn't notice the stones underneath.

Soon the trail disappeared into the base of the rock. Those ahead had been slowed by the climb, and the women coming from behind caught up with us. Hands gripping the rock, we slowly followed the others up the cliff. Along with our group of twenty-five from Hedangna, there were Bhotes (Tibetans) from the northern Arun Valley and Chetris (Hindus) from the south. Together, sixty or more people were making their way up the rock face.

In the West, we climb rocks with rope and protection. We wear soft rubber under our feet. We are on the rock, yet not on the rock. With these pilgrims I climbed to the Khembalung caves barefoot, with no rope. Perched on a tiny ledge, Jadu Prasad reached down to pull me over difficult sections. I clutched his hand as he hauled me up the cliff, not letting myself think about what he in turn was holding on to. At a particularly difficult part, one of the grandmothers looked at me with concern and suggested I go down. But then a man appeared with a twelve-foot piece of rope. He knelt above the difficult section and held the rope as I used it to climb up the crack.

Once, at a Quaker wedding I attended, the father of the groom talked about thin places, about places where one's nerve endings are bare. We take pilgrimages to thin places, to places where gods have made their mark on the land. As the legends of the hidden valleys make clear, these journeys are internal as much as they are external. How thin the place seems to us depends on who we are and where we come from; most important, it depends on what we bring and what we can relinquish in order to make our journey.

I often joined the women in the fields in Hedangna, helping with digging and planting and cutting and carrying, doing whatever I could to create something in common for us to share. Though I was slower and clumsier, they welcomed the free labor and perhaps the novelty of having me around. During breaks in the work, when we were gathered on a rock or under a tree, the women, old and young, would reach for my hands and rub their fingers slowly across my skin. They would turn over my hand and feel the palm, pulling the fingers up close to their eyes, and they would comment to each other on how smooth and white it was. Then they would hold up their own hands and feet, which were tough and dark, next to mine and shake their heads. They lived by their hands, they would say, and I lived by my head.

The women in Hedangna want skin like mine. They want some padding in their lives, want to be able to stay inside for a while and let their bodies become smooth and white and soft. I went to Hedangna because I wanted skin like theirs. I wanted its thickness and its toughness, a toughness that seemed to be a sign of an internal strength, a thickening from the inside that allowed them to get by without a lot of external support. Their dark, callused skin enabled them to walk through their lives barefoot, enduring, not avoiding, the sharpness and the pain encountered along the way.

I was raised in a world where the answer to a problem or the solution to pain was always out there, around the next corner, in the next place or next job or next year. I was educated away from my home, taught to believe there was more to be gained by moving forward then by staying put. I came to Hedangna, a community where people still farm the land their ancestors cleared eleven generations ago, because I wanted to learn what it took to stay at home. I wondered what life was like without the leather and the plastic. I came to Hedangna because I wanted to relearn what it meant to live from the inside, with my hands and my feet and my heart—because I wanted to re-member what their ways of living have never let them forget. And as I climbed the rock face to the Khembalung caves, I found myself entering one of the thinnest places I had ever been. [. . .]

During the whole trip, I felt an ache in my chest, a longing that would not go away. I thought there must be a place, some-where, where I could be held, here, no *here*, on the inside. If only I could get to that place, I was sure, the yearning would disappear. Now I realize that this feeling of aloneness is not something that ever goes away. It is always there, underneath the words spoken, inside my boots. It's what comes up in thin places. It's what you feel when the skin peels off your feet.

→>–<←

"I turn upon her at the end of it, and yell at her to be quiet—not to be a damn-fool girl, it was just a story, about a stupid little doll, and there she is, crying her eyes out as though she's been living in it. Tridib laughs and shakes me by the neck and tells me not to shout at her. Everyone lives in a story, he says, my grandmother, my father, his father, Lenin, Einstein, and lots of other names I hadn't heard of; they all lived in stories, because stories are all there are to live in."

—AMITAV GHOSH, The Shadow Lines

→>–<←

WENDELL BERRY
The Record · 1998

My old friend tells us how the country changed:
where the grist mill was on Cane Run,
now gone; where the peach orchard was,
gone too; where the Springport Road was, gone
beneath returning trees; how the creek ran three weeks
after a good rain, long ago, no more;
how when these hillsides first were plowed, the soil
was black and deep, no stones, and that was long ago;
where the wild turkeys roosted in the old days.

"You'd have to know this country mighty well
before I could tell you where."

And my young friend says: "Have him speak this
into a recorder. It is precious. It should be saved."
I know the panic of that wish to save
the vital knowledge of the old times, handed down,
for it is rising off the earth, fraying away
in the wind and the coming day.
As the machines come and the people go
the old names rise, chattering, and depart.

But knowledge of my own going into old time
tells me no. Because it must be saved,
do not tell it to a machine to save it.
That old man speaking you have heard
since your boyhood, since his prime, his voice
speaking out of lives long dead, their minds
speaking in his own, by winter fires, in fields and woods,
in barns while rain beat on the roofs
and wind shook the girders. Stay and listen
until he dies or you die, for death
is in this, and grief is in it. Live here
as one who knows these things. Stay, if you live;
listen and answer. Listen to the next one
like him, if there is to be one. Be
the next one like him, if you must.
Stay and wait. Tell your children. Tell them
to tell their children. As you depart

toward the coming light, turn back
and speak, as the creek steps downward
over the rocks, saying the same changing thing
in the same place as it goes.

When the record is made, the unchanging
word carried to a safe place
in a time not here, the assemblage
of minds dead and living, the loved lineage
dispersed, silent, turned away, the dead
dead at last, it will be too late.

"For when a nation loses its poets it loses access to the meaning of dwelling. When it loses the meaning of dwelling, it loses the means to build. By the same vicious logic, when it loses the means to build, dwelling itself loses its meaning. No amount of running water or safe wiring can of itself turn a house into a home, for when a nation ignores its poets it becomes a nation of the homeless."

—Robert Pogue Harrison, *Forest: A Shadow of Civilization*

Chapter 9: The Whole Individual

This chapter asks us to think like a social movement, and to consider the values taught in land conservation as a quiet form of civil disobedience that opposes the prevailing cultural forces of our times. Every successful social movement has achieved its goals by addressing the basic human condition. A fractured human being leads to a fractured society, and a whole individual is the seed for a pluralistic and engaged society. Thoreau's argument in Civil Disobedience *was that our society's consistent move away from the land and a simple life had enabled us to accept other contradictions, allowing us to believe one thing while acting out another. The conservation movement succeeds brilliantly in saving hundreds of thousands of acres of land each year, but somehow provides no broadly recognizable cultural counterpoint to America's otherwise materialistic society. The conservation movement is largely silent on the choices Americans make about how one should live.*

Is there no dissonance in saying that a movement is devoted to saving land but not devoted to fighting the consumption that destroys land? Is it possible that we are winning the battle while losing the war? In a world with a shared land ethic, conservation should be able to answer the question, how does its work afford average people the opportunity for more meaningful and whole lives?

→>◄←

"Now I see the secret of making of the best persons. It is to grow in the open air, and to eat and sleep with the earth."

—Walt Whitman, *Leaves of Grass*

"Most people are 'on' the world, not in it—have no conscious sympathy or relationship to anything about them—undiffused, separate, and rigidly alone like marbles of polished stone, touching but separate."

—JOHN MUIR, *journal entry*

✦

WENDELL BERRY
Conservation Is Good Work · 1992

However destructive may be the policies of the government and the methods and products of the corporations, the root of the problem is always to be found in private life. We must learn to see that every problem that concerns us as conservationists always leads straight to the question of how we live. The world is being destroyed, no doubt about it, by the greed of the rich and powerful. It is also being destroyed by popular demand. There are not enough rich and powerful people to consume the whole world; for that, the rich and powerful need the help of countless ordinary people. We acquiesce in the wastefulness and destructiveness of the national and global economics by acquiescing in the wastefulness and destructiveness of our own households and communities. If conservation is to have a hope of succeeding, then conservationists, while continuing their effort to change public life, are going to have to begin the effort to change private life as well.

The problems we are worried about are caused not just by other people but by ourselves. And this realization should lead directly to two more. The first is that solving these problems is not work merely for so-called environmental organizations and agencies but also for individuals, families, and local communities. We are used to hearing about turning off unused lights, putting a brick in the toilet tank, using water-saving shower heads, setting the thermostat low, sharing rides, and so forth—pretty dull stuff. But I'm talking about actual jobs of work that are interesting because they require intelligence and because they are accomplished in response to interesting questions: What are the principles of household economy, and how can they be applied under present circumstances? What are the principles of a neighborhood or a local economy, and how can they be applied under present circumstances? What do people already possess in their minds and bodies, in their families and neighborhoods, in their dwellings and in their local landscape, that can replace what is now being supplied by our consumptive and predatory so-called economy? What can we supply to ourselves cheaply or for nothing that we are now paying dearly for? To answer such questions requires more intelligence and involves more pleasure than all the technological breakthroughs of the last two hundred years.

"And did you get what you wanted from this life, even so? I did. And what did you want? To call myself beloved, to feel myself beloved on the earth."

—Raymond Carver, *Late Fragment*

"One of our problems today is that we are not well acquainted with the literature of the spirit. We're interested in the news of the day and the problems of the hour. . . . When you get to be older, and the concerns of the day have all been attended to, and you turn to the inner life—well, if you don't know where it is or what it is, you'll be sorry."

—JOSEPH CAMPBELL, *The Power of Myth*

→>—<←

JOANNA MACY
World as Lover, World as Self · 1993

To experience the world as an extended self and its story as our own extended story involves no surrender or eclipse of our individuality. The liver, leg, and lung that are "mine" are highly distinct from each other, thank goodness, and each has a distinctive role to play. The larger selfness we discover today is not an undifferentiated unity. Our recognition of this may be the third part of an unfolding of consciousness that began a long time ago, like the third movement of a symphony.

In the first movement, our infancy as a species, we felt no separation from the natural world around us. Trees, rocks, and plants surrounded us with a living presence as intimate and pulsing as our own bodies. In that primal intimacy, which anthropologists call "participation mystique," we were as one with our world as a child in the mother's womb.

Then self-consciousness arose and gave us distance on our world. We needed that distance in order to make decisions and strategies, in order to measure, judge and to monitor our judgments. With the emergence of free-will, the fall out of the Garden of Eden, the second movement began—the lonely and heroic journey of the ego. Nowadays, yearning to reclaim a sense of wholeness, some of us tend to disparage that movement of separation from nature, but it brought great gains for which we can be grateful. The distanced and observing eye brought us tools of science, and a priceless view of the vast, orderly intricacy of our world. The recognition of our individuality brought us trial by jury and the Bill of Rights.

Now, harvesting these gains, we are ready to return. The third movement begins. Having gained distance and sophistication of perception, we can turn and recognize who we have been all along. Now it can dawn on us: we are our world knowing itself. We can relinquish our separateness. We can come home again —and participate in our world in a richer, more responsible and poignantly beautiful way than before, in our infancy.

Because of the journey we undertook to distance ourselves from our world, it is no longer undifferentiated from us. It can appear to us now both as self and as lover. Relating to our world with the full measure of our being, we partake of the qualities of both. I think of a poem, "The Old Mendicant," by Vietnamese Zen master Thich Nhat Hanh. In it he evokes the long, wondrous evolutionary journey we all have made together, from which we are as inseparable as from our own selves. At the same time, it is a love song. Hear these lines, as if addressed to you.

Being rock, being gas, being mist, being Mind,
Being the mesons traveling among galaxies with the speed of light,

You have come here, my beloved one . . .
You have manifested yourself as trees, as grass, as butter-
flies, as single-celled beings, and as chrysanthemums;
but the eyes with which you looked at me this morning
tell me you have never died.

We have all gone that long journey, and now, richer for it, we
come home to our mutual belonging. We return to experience, as we never could before, that we are both the self of our
world and its cherished lover. We are not doomed to destroy it
by the cravings of the separate ego and the technologies it
fashioned. We can wake up to who we really are, and allow the
waters of the Rhine to flow clean once more, and the trees to
grow green along its banks.

→>-<-

HELEN AND SCOTT NEARING
Living the Good Life · 1954

We were seeking an affirmation, a way of conducting ourselves, of looking at the world and taking part in its activities
that would provide at least a minimum of those values which
we considered essential to the good life. As we saw it, such values must include: simplicity, freedom from anxiety and tension, an opportunity to be useful and to live harmoniously. [. . .]

Our second purpose was to make a living under conditions that
would preserve and enlarge joy in workmanship, would give a
sense of achievement, thereby promoting integrity and self

respect; would assure a large measure of self sufficiency . . . and make it easier to guarantee the solvency of the enterprise. . .

Our third aim was leisure during a considerable portion of the day, month or year, which might be devoted . . . to satisfying and fruitful association with one's fellows, and to individual and group efforts toward social improvement.

1. Do the best you can, whatever arises
2. Be at peace with yourself
3. Find a job you enjoy
4. Live in simple conditions; housing, food, clothing, get rid of clutter
5. Contact nature everyday; feel the earth under your feet
6. Take physical exercise through hard work; through gardening or walking
7. Don't worry; live one day at a time
8. Share something every day with someone else; if you live alone, write someone; give something away; help someone else
9. Take time to wonder at life and the world; see some humor in life when you can
10. Observe the one life in all things
11. Be kind to the creatures

GARY SNYDER
On the Path, Off the Trail · 1990

The truly experienced person, the refined person, *delights in the ordinary.* Such a person will find the tedious work around the house or office as full of challenge and play as any metaphor of mountaineering might suggest. I would say the real play is in the act of going totally off the trail—away from any trace of human or animal regularity aimed at some practical or spiritual purpose. One goes out onto the "trail that cannot be followed" which leads everywhere and nowhere, a limitless fabric of possibilities, elegant variations a millionfold on the same themes, yet each point unique. Every boulder on a talus slope is different, no two needles on a fir tree are identical. How could one part be more central, more important, than any other? One will never come onto the three-foot-high heaped-up nest of a Bushy-tailed Woodrat, made of twigs and stones and leaves, unless one plunges into the manzanita thickets. Strive hard! . . .

Our skills and works are but tiny reflections of the wild world that is innately and loosely orderly. There is nothing like stepping away from the road and heading into a new part of the watershed. Not for the sake of newness, but for the sense of coming home to our whole terrain. "Off the trail" is another name for the Way, and sauntering off the trail is the practice of the wild. That is also where—paradoxically—we do our best work. But we need paths and trails and will always be maintaining them. You first must be on the path, before you can turn and walk into the wild.

It is now often said (ever since Wendell Berry stated it so clearly and forcefully) that our ecological crisis is a crisis of character, not a political or social crisis. This said, we falter, for it remains unclear what, exactly, is the crisis of modern character; and since character is partly determined by culture, what, exactly, is the crisis of modern culture. Answers to these questions are not to be found in the writings of Thoreau, or Muir, or ecologists ("deep" or otherwise). Answers, always controversial, are found in the study of the Holocaust, the study of "primitive" peoples untouched by our madness, and in the study of the self.

Although the ecological crisis appears new (because it is now "news"), it is not new; only the scale and form are new. We lost the wild bit by bit for ten thousand years and forgave each loss and then forgot. Now we face the final loss. Although no other crisis in human history can match it, our commentary is strangely muted and sad, as though catastrophe was happening to us, not caused by us. Even the most knowledgeable and enlightened continue to eat food soaked in chemicals (herbicides, pesticides, and hormones), wear plastic clothes (our beloved polypropylene), buy Japanese (despite their annual slaughter of dolphins), and vote Republican—all the while blathering on in abstract language about our ecological crisis. This is denial, and behind denial is a rage, the most common emotion of my generation; but it is suppressed, and we remain silent in the face of evil.

Why is this rage a silent rage, a quiet impotent protest that doesn't extend beyond the confines of our private world? Why don't people speak out, why don't they *do* something? The courage and resistance shown by the Navajos at Big Mountain, by Polish workers, by blacks in South Africa, and, most extraordinarily, by Chinese students in Tiananmen Square render much of the environmental protest in America shallow and ineffective. With the exception of a few members of Earth First!, Sea Shepherd, and Greenpeace, we are a nation of environmental cowards. Why?

Effective protest is grounded in anger, and we are not (consciously) angry. Anger nourishes hope and fuels rebellion; it presumes a judgment, presumes how things ought to be and aren't, presumes a care. Emotion is still the best evidence of belief and value.

"But let's assume we now face the future with better intentions. The coming decades are bound to be difficult. We will have to replace a destructive economy of mindless expansion with one that consciously respects earthly limits and human scale. To begin doing that, we'll have to reevaluate some sacred ideas about ourselves. We'll have to give up our fetish for extreme individualism and rediscover public life. In doing so, we will surely rediscover public manners and some notion of the common good. We will have to tell some people what they can and cannot do with their land."

—JAMES HOWARD KUNSTLER, *The Geography of Nowhere*

"You're thinking of revolution as a great all-or-nothing. I think of it as one more morning in a muggy cotton field, checking the undersides of leaves to see what's been there, figuring out what to do that won't clear a path for worse problems next week. Right now that's what I do. You ask why I'm not afraid of loving and losing, and that's my answer. Wars and elections are both too big and too small to matter in the long run. The daily work—that goes on, it adds up. It goes into the ground, into crops, into children's bellies and their bright eyes. Good things don't get lost. I've decided: the very least you can do in your life is to figure out what you hope for. And the most you can do is live inside that hope. Not admire it from a distance but live right in it, under its roof."

—BARBARA KINGSOLVER, *Animal Dreams*

ROBERT MICHAEL PYLE
The Thunder Tree · 1993

Had it not been for the High Line Canal, the vacant lots I knew, the scruffy park, I'm not at all certain I would have been a biologist. I might have become a lawyer, or even a Lutheran. The total immersion in nature that I found in my special spots baptized me in a faith that never wavered, but it was a matter of happenstance too. It was the place that made me.

How many people grow up with such windows on the world? Fewer and fewer, I fear, as metropolitan habitats disappear and rural ones blend into the urban fringe. The number of people living with little hint of nature in their lives is very large and growing. This isn't good for us. If the penalty of an ecological education is to live in a world of wounds, as Aldo Leopold said, then green spaces like these are the bandages and the balm. And if the penalty of ecological ignorance is still more wounds, then the unschooled need them even more. To gain the solace of nature, we all must connect deeply. Few ever do.

In the long run, this mass estrangement from things natural bodes ill for the care of the earth. If we are to forge new links to the land, we must resist the extinction of experience. We must save not only the wilderness but the vacant lots, the ditches as well as the canyonlands, and the woodlots along with the old growth. We must become believers in the world.

→>-<-

LINDA HOGAN
Dwellings · *1995*

In the background, the sweat lodge structure stands. Birds are on it. It is still skeletal. A woman and man are beginning to place old rugs and blankets over the bent cottonwood frame. A great fire is already burning, and the lava stones that will be the source of heat for the sweat are being fired in it. [. . .]

By late afternoon we are ready, one at a time, to enter the enclosure. The hot lava stones are placed inside. They remind us of earth's red and fiery core, and of the spark inside all life. After the flap, which serves as a door, is closed, water is poured over the stones and the hot steam rises around us. In a sweat lodge ceremony, the entire world is brought inside the enclosure.

The soft odor of smoking cedar accompanies this arrival. It is all called in. The animals come from the warm and sunny distances. Water from dark lakes is there. Wind. Young, lithe willow branches bent overhead remember their lives rooted in ground, the sun their leaves took in. They remember that minerals and water rose up their trunks, and birds nested in their leaves, and that planets turned above their brief, slender lives. The thunderclouds travel in from far regions of earth. Wind arrives from the four directions. It has moved through caves and breathed through our bodies. It is the same air elk have inhaled, air that passed through the lungs of a grizzly bear. The sky is there, with all the stars whose lights we see long after the stars themselves have gone back to nothing. It is a place grown intense and holy. It is a place of immense community and of humbled solitude; we sit together in our aloneness and speak, one at a time, our deepest language of need, hope, loss, and survival. We remember that all things are connected.

Remembering this is the purpose of the ceremony. It is part of a healing and restoration. It is the mending of a broken connection between us and the rest. The participants in a ceremony say the words "All my relations" before and after we pray; those words create a relationship with other people, with animals, with the land. To have health it is necessary to keep all these relations in mind. The intention of a ceremony is to put a person back together by restructuring the human mind. This reorganization is accomplished by a kind of inner map, a geography of the human spirit and the rest of the world. We make whole our broken-off pieces of self and world. Within ourselves, we bring together the fragments of our lives in a sacred act of renewal, and we reestablish our connections with others. The ceremony is a point of return. It takes us toward the place of balance, our place in the community of all things. It is an event that sets us back upright. But it is not a finished thing. The real ceremony begins where the formal one ends, when we take up a new way, our minds and hearts filled with the vision of earth that holds us within it, in compassionate relationship to and with our world.

We speak. We sing. We swallow water and breathe smoke. By the end of the ceremony, it is as if skin contains land and birds. The places within us have become filled. As inside the enclosure of the lodge, the animals and ancestors move into the human body, into skin and blood. The land merges with us. The stones come to dwell inside the person. Gold rolling hills take up residence, their tall grasses blowing. The red light of canyons is there. The black skies of night that wheel above our heads come to live inside the skull. We who easily grow apart from the world are returned to the great store of life all around us, and there is the deepest sense of being at home here in this intimate kinship. There is no real aloneness. There is solitude and the nurturing silence that is relationship with ourselves, but even then we are part of something larger.

After a sweat lodge ceremony, the enclosure is abandoned. Quieter now, we prepare to drive home. We pack up the kettles, the coffeepot. The prayer ties are placed in nearby trees. Some of the other people prepare to go to work, go home, or cook a dinner. We drive. Everything returns to ordinary use. A spider weaves a web from one of the cottonwood poles to another. Crows sit inside the framework. It's evening. The crickets are singing. All my relations.

"This is the joy of life, the being used up for a purpose recognized by yourself as a mighty one; being a force of nature instead of a feverish, selfish little clod of ailments and grievance, complaining that the world will not devote itself to making you happy.

"I am of the opinion that my life belongs to the community, and as long as I live, it is my privilege to do for it whatever I can. I want to be thoroughly used up when I die, for the harder I work, the more I live.

"Life is no 'brief candle' to me. It is a sort of splendid torch which I have got hold of for a moment, and I want to make it burn as brightly as possible before handing it on to future generations."

—George Bernard Shaw

✢✤✤

Antoine de Saint-Exupéry
The Little Prince · 1971

It was then that the fox appeared.

"Good morning," said the fox.

"Good morning," the little prince responded politely, although when he turned around he saw nothing.

"I am right here," the voice said, "under the apple tree."

"Who are you?" asked the little prince, and added, "You are very pretty to look at."

"I am a fox," the fox said.

"Come and play with me," proposed the little prince. "I am so unhappy."

"I cannot play with you," the fox said. "I am not tamed."

"Ah! Please excuse me," said the little prince.

But, after some thought, he added:

"What does that mean—'tame'?"

"You do not live here," said the fox. "What is it that you are looking for?"

"I am looking for men," said the little prince. "What does that mean—'tame'?"

"Men," said the fox. "They have guns, and they hunt. It is very disturbing. They also raise chickens. These are their only interests. Are you looking for chickens?"

"No," said the little prince. I am looking for friends. What does that mean—'tame'?"

"It is an act too often neglected," said the fox. "It means to establish ties."

" 'To establish ties'?"

"Just that," said the fox. "To me, you are still nothing more than a little boy who is just like a hundred thousand other little boys. And I have no need of you. And you, on your part, have no need of me. To you, I am nothing more than a fox like a hundred thousand other foxes. But if you tame me, then we shall need each other. To me, you will be unique in the world. To you, I shall be unique in all the world . . ." [. . .]

"My life is very monotonous," [the fox] said. "I hunt chickens; men hunt me. All the chickens are just alike, and all the men are just alike. And, in consequence, I am a little bored. But if you tame me, it will be as if the sun came to shine on my life. I shall know the sound of a step that will be different from all the others. Other steps send me hurrying back underneath the ground. Yours will call me, like music, out of my burrow. And then look: you see the grain-fields down yonder? I do not eat bread. Wheat is of no use to me. The wheat fields have nothing to say to me. And that is sad. But you have hair that is the color of gold. Think how wonderful that will be when you have tamed me! The grain, which is also golden, will bring me back the thought of you. And I shall love to listen to the wind in the wheat . . ."

The fox gazed at the little prince, for a long time.

"Please—tame me!" he said.

"I want to, very much," the little prince replied. "But I have not much time. I have friends to discover, and a great many things to understand."

"One only understands the things that one tames," said the fox. "Men have no more time to understand anything. They buy things all ready made at the shops. But there is no shop anywhere where one can buy friendship, and so men have no friends any more. If you want a friend, tame me . . ."

"What must I do, to tame you?" asked the little prince.

"You must be very patient," replied the fox. "First you will sit down at a little distance from me—like that—in the grass. I shall look at you out of the corner of my eye, and you will say nothing. Words are the source of misunderstandings. But you will sit a little closer to me, every day . . ."

The next day the little prince came back.

"It would have been better to come back at the same hour," said the fox. "If, for example, you come at four o'clock in the afternoon, then at three o'clock I shall begin to be happy. I shall feel happier and happier as the hour advances. At four o'clock, I shall already be worrying and jumping about. I shall show you how happy I am! But if you come at just any time, I shall never know at what hour my heart is to be ready to greet you . . . One must observe the proper rites."

"What is a rite?" asked the little prince.

"Those also are actions too often neglected," said the fox. "They are what make one day different from other days, one hour from other hours. There is a rite, for example, among my hunters. Every Thursday they dance with the village girls. So Thursday is a wonderful day for me! I can take a walk as far as the vineyards. But if the hunters danced at just any time, every day would be like every other day, and I should never have any vacation at all."

So the little prince tamed the fox. And when the hour of his departure drew near—

"Ah," said the fox, "I shall cry."

"It is your own fault," said the little prince. "I never wished you any sort of harm; but you wanted me to tame you . . ."

"Yes, that is so," said the fox.

"Then it has done you no good at all!"

"It has done me good," said the fox, "because of the color of the wheat fields." And then he added:

"Go and look again at the roses. You will understand now that yours is unique in all the world. Then come back to say goodbye to me, and I will make you a present of a secret." [. . .]

And he went back to meet the fox.

"Goodbye," he said.

"Goodbye," said the fox. "And now here is my secret, a very simple secret: It is only with the heart that one can see rightly; what is essential is invisible to the eye."

"What is essential is invisible to the eye," the little prince repeated, so that he would be sure to remember.

"It is the time you have wasted for your rose that makes your rose so important."

"It is the time I have wasted for my rose—" said the little prince, so that he would be sure to remember.

"Men have forgotten this truth," said the fox. "But you must not forget it. You become responsible, forever, for what you have tamed. You are responsible for your rose . . ."

"I am responsible for my rose," the little prince repeated, so that he would be sure to remember.

→>—<←

WENDELL BERRY
Speech to Organic Growers · 1998

Now, having completed this very formidable list of the problems and difficulties, fears and fearful hopes that lie ahead of us, I am relieved to see that I have been preparing myself all along to end by saying something cheerful. What I have been talking about is the possibility of renewing human respect for this earth and all the good, useful, and beautiful things that come from it. I have made it clear, I hope, that I don't think this respect can be adequately enacted or conveyed by tipping our hats to nature or by representing natural loveliness in art or by prayers of thanksgiving or by preserving tracts of wilderness —although I recommend all those things. The respect I mean can be given only by using well the world's goods that are given to us. This good use, which renews respect—which is the only currency, so to speak, of respect—also renews our pleasure. The callings and disciplines that I have spoken of as the domestic arts are stationed all along the way from the farm to the prepared dinner, from the forest to the dinner table, from stewardship of the land to hospitality to friends and strangers. These arts are as demanding and gratifying, as instructive and as pleasing as the so-called "fine arts." To learn them, to practice them, to honor and reward them is, I believe, the work that is our profoundest calling. Our reward is that they will enrich our lives and make us glad. [. . .]

We are involved now in a profound failure of imagination. Most of us cannot imagine the wheat beyond the bread, or the farmer beyond the wheat, or the farm beyond the farmer, or the history (human or natural or sacred) beyond the farm. Most people cannot imagine the forest and the forest economy that produced their houses and furniture and paper, or the landscapes, the streams, and the weather that fill their pitchers and bathtubs and swimming pools with water. Most people appear to assume that when they have paid their money for these things they have entirely met their obligations. And that is, in fact, the conventional economic assumption. The problem is that it is possible to starve under the rule of the conventional economic assumption; some people are starving now under the rule of that assumption.

Money does not bring forth food. Neither does the technology of the food system. Food comes from nature and from the work of people. If the supply of food is to be continuous for a long time, then people must work in harmony with nature. That means that people must find the right answers to a lot of hard practical questions. The same applies to forestry and the possibility of a continuous supply of timber.

People grow the food that people eat. People produce the lumber that people use. People care properly or improperly for the forests and the farms that are the sources of those goods. People are necessarily at both ends of the process. The economy, always obsessed with its need to sell products, thinks obsessively and exclusively of the consumer. It mostly takes for granted or ignores those who do the damaging or the restorative and preserving work of agriculture and forestry. The economy pays poorly for this work, with the unsurprising result that the work is mostly done poorly. But here we must ask a very realistic economic question: Can we afford to have this work done poorly? Those of us who know something about land stewardship know that we cannot afford to pay poorly for it, because that means simply that we will not get it. And we know that we cannot afford land use without land stewardship.

One way we could describe the task ahead of us is by saying that we need to enlarge the consciousness and the conscience of the economy. Our economy needs to know—and care—

what it is doing. This is revolutionary, of course, if you have a taste for revolution, but it is also a matter of common sense. How could anybody seriously object to the possibility that the economy might eventually come to know what it is doing?

→>⤙

RALPH WALDO EMERSON
Self-Reliance · *1841*

There is a time in every man's education when he arrives at the conviction that envy is ignorance; that imitation is suicide; that he must take himself for better, for worse, as his portion; that though the wide universe is full of good, no kernel of nourishing corn can come to him but through his toil bestowed to him on that plot of ground which is given to him to till. The power which resides in him is new in nature, and none but he knows what that is which he can do, nor does he know until he has tried. [. . .] Virtues are, in the popular estimate, rather the exception than the rule. There is the man *and* his virtues. Men do what is called a good action, as some piece of courage or charity, much as they would pay a fine in expiation of daily nonappearance on parade. Their works are done as an apology or extenuation of their living in the world,—as invalids and the insane pay a high board. Their virtues are penances. I do not wish to expiate, but to live. My life is for itself and not for a spectacle.

Chapter 10: The Whole Community

This final chapter explores the complete interconnectedness of life, how everyday human problems spring from and contribute to the common earthly problems of the planet, how cultural diversity relies on natural diversity, how the needs of the city hinge on the success of the village. It asks us to apply the laws of ecology, as values as much as science, to the workings of our most successful human communities. In asking us to view all life—and all neighbors—as part of the same family, it shows us the first glimpse of a nation with a land ethic. The concept of community "wholeness," the vibrancy of a community's ecology, economy, people, and social institutions, assumes minimal boundaries and the existence of a land-based culture. A human community grounded in nature takes on positive characteristics that an interest-based community cannot possibly attain. The former is characterized by mutual aid, interdependence, and relationship, while the latter is defined largely by financial exchange.

What can an individual's connection to land tell us about the possibilities for a community's connection to land? What makes a land-based community different from an interest-based community? Why does biodiversity need cultural diversity? Why should city ecology be a concern to the land conservation movement? How might the conservation movement apply these concepts of "wholeness" to our land-saving projects and to our mission?

→>—<←

"Community, then, is an indispensable term in any discussion of the connection between people and land. A healthy community is a form that includes all the local things that are connected by the larger, ultimately mysterious form of the Creation. In speaking of community, then, we are speaking of a complex connection not only among human beings or between humans and their homeland but also between the human economy and nature, between forest or prairie and field or orchard, and between troublesome creatures and pleasant ones. *All* neighbors are included."

—WENDELL BERRY, *Conservation and Local Economy*

→>-<←

EVAN EISENBERG
Ecology of Eden · 1998

There are feelings our forebears got in wilderness which we get only in great cities. The feeling of being lost in something huge, something other, something that is not of your own making and that does not give a hang whether you live or die —and yet not so lost that you have no hope of finding your way. Of being alone and invisible, far from the eye of family and friends. Of being up against hardship and danger, but having the skills to surmount them. The feeling that anything can happen—that at any moment a magus may appear and transform you into a prince or a fleabitten cur. That the elevator into which you now step may take you to heaven or hell.

To say this last thing is to say that the city is what wilderness was—a world-pole. In times past, young men braved the wilderness to prove their manhood. The wild world-pole was the place of passage. Today the other world-pole, the big city, is where young men and women go to prove themselves, to make their fortune and win their mates. [. . .]

Wilderness holds the germ of the city, of every city that has been and every city that will ever be. Not only the biological stuff of the city, but the very traits that define its cityhood—the division of labor, the honeycombed thickness, the tangled exchange of goods and information—have their origin in wildness. And without wilderness to do the global housekeeping, no future city will long survive.

The city, for its part, contains in its stones and flesh and frenzy the memory not only of the wilderness from which it was once hewn, and of the wildernesses that are still chipped away to make it grow, but of the many earlier and huger wildernesses that helped push evolution in this peculiar direction. The city may even be said to hold the germ of future wildernesses. For without big, vital, and well-ordered cities, the tide of human population must soon overwhelm whatever wilderness is left.

"Like all treasures of the mind, perception can be split into infinitely small fractions without losing its quality. The weeds in a city lot convey the same lesson as the redwoods."

—ALDO LEOPOLD, *A Sand County Almanac*

Daniel Kemmis
The Good City and the Good Life · 1995

Why would anyone even imagine that something like the Farmers' Market could play a role in mending a suffering democracy? Fixated as we are on "important" state and national issues such as term limits, campaign finance reform, crime, health care, and welfare reform, this suggestion seems at first to be merely frivolous. But, in fact, none of the other paths to reform on which people expend so much energy will reverse the decline of democracy, and none of the policies that we enact to deal with pressing problems such as poverty, racism, environmental damage, and drug and alcohol abuse will do any more than slow the worsening of these evils until we begin to understand the political importance of events like the Farmers' Market. No amount of reforming institutions that are widely and rightly perceived to be beyond human scale will heal our political culture until we begin to pay attention once again to democracy as a human enterprise. Without healing the human base of politics, we will not restore democracy itself. One thing alone will give us the capacity to heal our politics and to confront the problems and opportunities that politics must address. That one thing is a deeply renewed human experience of citizenship.

To redeem the democratic potential of citizenship, we need to take an entirely fresh look at its essential features. One of those, surprisingly, is citizenship's intimate connection to the city, from which both its name and its fundamental human significance derive. What makes a city civilized is something that is also absolutely fundamental to citizenship: in both instances, the basic feature is the human element. In the case of citizenship, this facet will make its claim most clearly if we allow it to appear, not where we might expect to find it, in governmental institutions, or in theories or documents, but in the most unassumingly human settings. [. . .]

The reason is that the city itself is alive, and it is in its own fullness of life that it has the capacity to become humanly livable and humanly fulfilling. If the story of the Farmers' Market is to reveal any fruitful clues about healing our politics, we need to understand how the rounding off, the simple search for a little greater wholeness that the market represents, is reflected in the greater life of the city as a political institution. This fundamental connection between human wholeness and livability and the wholeness and life of the city are all contained in Gertrud's choice of the word "civilized."

When I think of Gertrud's experience growing up in Germany, I try to imagine which features of the cities she knew might be reflected and recalled for her here at Missoula's Farmers' Market. What comes to mind is a description of the good city put forward by a group of architects, led by Christopher Alexander:

When we look at the most beautiful towns and cities of the past, we are always impressed by a feeling that they are somehow organic. . . . Each of these towns grew as a whole, under its own laws of wholeness . . . and we can feel this wholeness not only at the largest scale, but in every detail: in the restaurants, in the sidewalks, in the houses, shops, markets, roads, parks, gardens and walls. Even in the balconies and ornaments.

What is so refreshing about Alexander's approach is that he speaks of this wholeness in incremental terms that bring it within human reach. Certainly if we look around any of our large cities today, the picture of wholeness that Alexander shows us seems remote, and if we imagine trying to bring anything like it about by a grand act of will, we must feel immediately defeated. Even here in Missoula, a modest city of some sixty thousand people, any dream of achieving some comprehensive sense of wholeness in the city at large that might mirror what I see around me here at the market would leave me or any of my neighbors in despair.

But Alexander's approach is to remind us of the connection between healing and wholeness, arguing that we have countless opportunities to take small healing steps to move the city in the direction of wholeness. "Every increment of construction," he writes, "must be made in such a way as to heal the city." While the ultimate objective is to realize the wholeness of the city itself, each act of healing has the potential to create smaller pockets of wholeness. According to Alexander, "Every new act of construction has just one basic obligation: it must create a continuous structure of wholes around itself."

These architectural insights about the organic nature of the good city, and about wholeness and healing, carry the promise of a much broader healing than Alexander imagines. Our efforts to address such profound problems as poverty, racism, drug and alcohol abuse, and teenage murders and suicides will continue to fail until we recognize, as Alexander has done, the central importance of wholeness, healing, and health as touchstones of the good city. Those problems can only be solved by a healthy, effective polity. Yet the epidemic dysfunctions in the body politic that Jerry exemplifies—the alienation, despair, and cynicism that are literally destroying democracy—cannot be healed except by nurturing the deeply human aspiration toward health and wholeness. Only citizenship can save politics, and only relatively whole people are capable of reclaiming the human meaning of citizenship from the rubble of a political culture inhabited largely by sullen "taxpayers." Yet there is every reason to believe that the wholeness of the city and of its citizens are utterly dependent upon each other—that neither is possible without the other. This circularity must not be taken as one more excuse for despair. Rather, it should encourage us to bring change within human reach by broadening Alexander's step-at-a-time approach from the physical city to the political culture that is the city's larger self. [. . .]

The expanding awareness of the interdependence of city and suburb establishes a logical plumb line that inevitably leads to the recognition that not only must central cities and their suburbs acknowledge their combined wholeness if they are to thrive and prosper, but that they in turn must understand their organic relatedness to the surrounding countryside. So, for example, Mayor Jerry Abramson has insisted that Louisville begin exploring how the long-term viability of that city might depend upon the economic health of the hundreds of small towns for which Louisville serves as the hub. So Berlin has asked the German Bundestag to formally recognize and allow the city to pursue its natural connectedness to its surrounding region, as Beijing had recognized Hong Kong's relationship with Guangzhou. So every lesson I had ever learned as mayor led me to argue to the secretary of agriculture that the best favor he could do for "rural America" would be to meet with the secretary of housing and urban development and the secretary of transportation and agree to dismantle all the national programs that had made "rural America," "urban America," and "suburban America" think they could prosper in isolation from one another.

→>-<←

LOUIS FISCHER
The Life of Mahatma Gandhi · 1950

[*Editor's note:* Khadi is the tradition started by Gandhi for Indians to make their own cloth for clothing.]

In 1924, 1925, 1926, and 1927, the popularizing of khadi possessed Gandhi's mind. Each issue of the weekly *Young India* devoted several pages to lists of persons and the exact number of yards of yarn they had spun. Some spinners donated the yarn to the fund which gave it to villagers for weaving, others wove their own. Gandhi's Sabarmati Ashram was manufacturing simple spinning wheels, but in 1926 the manager announced that they had more orders than they could fill. Schools were giving courses in spinning. At Congress meetings, members would open a small box like a violin case, take out a collapsible spinning wheel, and spin noiselessly through-out the proceedings. Gandhi had set the fashion.

Some of Gandhi's closest friends accused him of khadi extremism; he exaggerated the possibility of restoring India's village industries and overestimated the benefits that might accrue even if he were successful; this was the machine age; all his energy, wisdom, and holiness would not avail to turn back the clock.

"A hundred and fifty years ago," Gandhi replied, "we manu-factured all our cloth. Our women spun fine yarns in their own cottages, and supplemented the earnings of their husbands. . . . India requires nearly thirteen yards of cloth per head per year. She produces, I believe, less than half the amount. India grows all the cotton she needs. She exports several million bales of cotton to Japan and Lancashire and receives much of it back in manufactured calico, although she is capable of producing all the cloth and all the yarn necessary for supplying her wants by hand-weaving and hand-spinning. . . . The spinning wheel was presented to the nation for giving occupation to the millions who had, at least for four months of the year, nothing to do. . . . We send out of India sixty crores [six hundred million] (more or less) of rupees for cloth. . . ."

Many intellectuals sneered at khadi. The stuff was coarse, they said. "Monotonous white shrouds," some mocked. "The livery of our freedom," Jawatharlal Nehru replied. "I regard the spin-ning wheel as a gateway to my spiritual salvation," Gandhi said.

Gandhi was trying to bridge brain and brawn, to unite city and town, to link rich and poor. What greater service could he perform for a divided country and an atomized civilization? To help the underdog, Gandhi taught, you must understand him, and to understand him you must at least sometimes work as he does. Spinning was an act of love, another channel of communication. It was also a method of organization. "Any single district that can be fully organized for khaddar is, if it is also trained for suffering, ready for civil disobedience." Thus, khadi would lead to home-rule.

Gandhi asked townspeople and villagers to spend an hour a day at the wheel. "It affords a pleasant variety and recreation after hard toil." Spinning does not replace other reforms; it is in addition to them. But he stressed them less than spinning.

"For me," Gandhi reiterated, "nothing in the political world is more important than the spinning wheel." One of India's greatest intellectuals, with a brain as keen as Gandhi's and as habitually skeptical as Gandhi was normally naive, enthusiastically supported the Mahatma's khadi contentions. Chakravarty Rajagopalachari, the famous Madras lawyer, was second only to Gandhi in his sanguine expectations from the nationwide use of homespun. "Khadi work is the only true political program before the country," he declared on April 6, 1926, in the textile-mill city of Ahmedabad. "You are living in a great city. You do not really know the amount of poverty that has overtaken the country called India. As a matter of fact, in India there are thousands and tens of thousands of villages where men do not get more than 2½ rupees a month. There is no use shedding tears for them if we won't wear a few yards of khadi which they have manufactured and want us to buy so that they may find a meal. If our hearts were not made of stone we would all be wearing khadi. Khadi means employment for the poor and freedom for India. Britain holds India because it is a fine market for Lancashire. . . ."

Motilal Nehru also took to wearing khadi; he peddled it in the streets as Gandhi did. Intellectuals might scoff, but khadi began to have a fascination for them, and from the mid-1920's, homespun became the badge of the Indian nationalist. A propagandist for independence would no more dream of going into a village in foreign clothes or foreign cloth or even in Indian mill cloth than he would think of speaking English at a peasant meeting. Apart from its economic value, which has not proved decisive, homespun was Gandhi's peculiar contribution to the education of political India: he made it physically conscious of poor, uneducated, non-political India. Khadi was an adventure in identification between leadership and nation. Gandhi was prescribing for a disease which plagued independent India and most independent countries. He knew that the tragedy of India's history was the canyon between the gold-silver-silk-brocade-jewel-elephant splendor of her palaces and the animal poverty of her hovels; at the bottom of the canyon lay the debris of empires and the bones of millions of their victims.

+>-<+

"Living in a place—the notion has been around for decades and usually been dismissed as provincial, backward, dull, and possibly reactionary. But new dynamics are at work. The mobility that has characterized American life is coming to a close. As Americans begin to stay put, it may give us the first opening in over a century to give participatory democracy another try."

—GARY SNYDER, *A Place in Space*

"The important thing is to identify with something or some things beyond the self. Actually, each is part of the whole. The immediate task is first to grasp the universal truth and the second to act upon it. Part of the essential process . . . is the maintenance at one and the same time of the self-respect and dignity of the individual and the responsibility which one has for other individuals, for the community, and . . . for the improvement of the environment."

—Scott Nearing, *The Making of a Radical*

-+->-<-+-

Gary Snyder
Coming into the Watershed · 1992

An economics of scale can be seen in the watershed/bioregion/city-state model. Imagine a Renaissance-style city-state facing out on the Pacific with its bioregional hinterland reaching to the headwaters of all the streams that flow through its bay. The San Francisco/valley rivers/Shasta headwaters bio-city-region! I take some ideas along these lines from Jane Jacobs's tantalizing book, *Cities and the Wealth of Nations* (New York: Random House, 1984), in which she argues that the city, not the nation-state, is the proper locus of an economy, and then that the city is always to be understood as being one with the hinterland.

Such a non-nationalistic idea of community, in which commitment to pure place is paramount, cannot be ethnic or racist. Here is perhaps the most delicious turn that comes out of thinking about politics from the standpoint of place: anyone of any race, language, religion, or origin is welcome, as long as they live well on the land. The great Central Valley region does not prefer English over Spanish or Japanese or Hmong. If it had any preferences at all, it might best like the languages it heard for thousands of years, such as Maidu or Miwok, simply because it's used to them. Mythically speaking, it will welcome whoever chooses to observe the etiquette, express the gratitude, grasp the tools, and learn the songs that it takes to live there.

This sort of future culture is available to whoever makes the choice, regardless of background. It need not require that a person drop his or her Buddhist, Jewish, Christian, animist, atheist, or Muslim beliefs but simply add to that faith or philosophy a sincere nod in the direction of the deep value of the natural world and the subjecthood of nonhuman beings. A culture of place will be created that will include the "United States," and go beyond that to an affirmation of the continent, the land itself, Turtle Island. We could be showing Southeast Asian and South American newcomers the patterns of the rivers, the distant hills, saying, "It is not only that you are now living in the United States. You are living in this great landscape. Please get to know these rivers and mountains, and be welcome here." Euro-Americans, Asian Americans, African Americans can—if they wish—become "born-again" natives of Turtle Island. In doing so we also might even (eventually) win some respect from our Native American predecessors, who are still here and still trying to teach us where we are.

Watershed consciousness and bioregionalism is not just environmentalism, not just a means toward resolution of social and economic problems, but a move toward resolving both nature and society with the practice of a profound citizenship in both the natural and the social worlds. If the ground can be our common ground, we can begin to talk to each other (human and nonhuman) once again.

✦

WENDELL BERRY
The Hidden Wound · 1989

There is no safety in belonging to the select few, for minority people or anybody else. If we are looking for insurance against want and oppression, we will find it only in our neighbors' prosperity and good will and, beyond that, in the good health of our worldly places, our homelands. If we were sincerely looking for a place of safety, for real security and success, then we would begin to turn to our communities—and not the communities simply of our human neighbors, but also of the water, earth, air, the plants and animals, all the creatures with whom our local life is shared. We would be looking too for another kind of freedom. Our present idea of freedom is only the freedom to do as we please: to sell ourselves for a high salary, a home in the suburbs, and idle weekends. But that is a freedom dependent upon affluence, which is in turn dependent upon the rapid consumption of exhaustible supplies. The other kind of freedom is the freedom to take care of ourselves and of each other. The freedom of affluence opposes and contradicts the freedom of community life. Our place of safety can only be the community, and not just one community, but many of them everywhere. Upon that depends all that we still claim to value: freedom, dignity, health, mutual help and affection, undestructive pleasure, and the rest. Human life, as most of us still would like to define it, is community life.

➻➤◅◅

"I once asked a teacher to describe how community life supports one's individual awakening. He told me it is like putting a handful of jagged-edge stones into a gem tumbler and turning on the machine. After sufficient tumbling, the stones emerge polished and sparkling—free of their rough edges. He said one has to realize that the stones become precious gems by rubbing up against one another in a rather intense environment."

—INSIGHT MEDITATION SOCIETY

➻➤◅◅

EDDY L. HARRIS
Solo Faces · *1997*

On that evening, whether or not I was the only fisherman, I was certainly the only black person on that stream, in those mountains, in the great state of Utah. Surely this is an exaggeration, and yet through hyperbole I suddenly realize it has been on my mind now for many years, this peculiar fact that whenever I find myself in nature—camping beside a dry creekbed in Montana, cross-country skiing in northern Vermont, hiking a bit of the Appalachian Trail—mine is nearly always the only black face around.

This is something that other black outdoorsmen have been

quietly puzzling over for years. My new friend Jean Ellis, for example, is an emergency room doctor from Billings, Montana. He's also an accomplished alpinist, and he's black. Ellis has attempted Everest and has climbed Cho Oyu in the Himalayas, distinguishing himself as the first black American to climb above 8,000 meters. "In 15 years," he says, "I've yet to meet another black climber in any country on any trip. And when I ask my other climbing friends how many blacks they've seen, they come up with one black climber a year. Maybe."

The same could be said of caving, kayaking, scuba diving, orienteering, surfing, hang-gliding, bouldering, birding, and just about any other intense wilderness pastime I can think of this side of hunting and fishing. Likewise, there's a conspicuous absence of black voices in the world of outdoor literature —not only black voices, but the voices of people of color in general. And with few exceptions, American environmentalism has always been a movement of monochrome white. The major environmental groups have long been aware of this problem, and during the early nineties, many made a conscientious effort to recruit nonwhites and to take up the cause of "environmental racism" (which charges, among other things, that industrialists have disproportionately located toxic dumps in minority neighborhoods). Yet lately the major American environmental groups have largely abandoned these efforts— which could perhaps be taken as a tacit acknowledgment of the wide gulf that separates white environmentalism from other shades of green.

But is this curious apartheid to be understood as a reality, or merely a perception of a reality? If you were to take only the images offered by television as a cue, you'd get the impression that blacks nowadays do just about everything everybody else does in America; there are black lawyers, black detectives, black ER docs, even black golfers, for godsakes. Blacks are everywhere to be found—everywhere, that is, but in the great outdoors. You don't see them bouncing through the Australian outback in the latest sport-utility wagon. You don't see them guzzling a sweat-beaded can of Coors Light against a backdrop of Rocky Mountain alpenglow. [. . .]

It's hard to tell, within this chicken-and-egg scenario, which comes first: the not being invited to the party and therefore not showing up, or the assumption that blacks party so differently that they need not be invited.

Still, it's a tricky thing for me to talk about this subject. For if it's true that blacks don't sail, don't surf, don't hike, what does it imply? That we don't like sunshine and spectacular scenery? That we harbor some deep-seated dread of water and snow? That we have an aversion to crisp, clean air?

And then, too, if there's a general rule about blacks in the outdoors, what do we make of the exceptions that are to be found just about everywhere, past and present? What about the prominent historical example of Matthew Henson, the noted black explorer who accompanied Robert E. Peary on numerous expeditions and, though Peary's exploration claims are contested, is still thought by many to have been the first person to stand at the North Pole? [. . .]

If the wilderness were not such a formidable place, we would not venerate the Indian tribes and the mountain folk and the frontiersmen and the cowboys who "tamed" the West and carved out a life from its harshness, nor would we seek to emulate them in tests of outdoor skill and courage. But concerning the challenges of nature, black Americans have an added element to deal with, one that white Americans can't fully fathom and that African-Americans are perhaps just beginning to come to terms with.

The black writer Evelyn C. White defined this challenge eloquently in an essay for the *San Francisco Chronicle* a few years ago. "It is not the sky or the trees or the creeks that have harmed us, but rather the people we have encountered along the way," she wrote. "Ask yourself why a black woman would find solace under the sun knowing that her great-great-grandmothers had toiled in brutal, blistering heat for slave-masters. It's no mystery to me why millions of African-Americans fled the 'pastoral South' for the grit and grime of northern cities."

The point, of course, is that historically bad things have happened to black people in the outdoors. If we choose to conjure them up, our associations with the woods can easily run in the direction of bloodhounds, swinging hemp ropes, and cracker Wizards in Klan bedsheets. And those associations, I think, play a large though largely unspoken role in this whole question.

This fear is not confined to the distant past.

+>-<+

"We all live in the city. We all live in the country. Both are second nature to us . . . to do right by nature and people in the country, one has to do right by them in the city as well, for the two seem always to find in each other their own image."

—WILLIAM CRONON, *Nature's Metropolis*

✦✦✦

RACHEL L. BAGBY
A Power of Numbers · 1989

The invitation said we would "discuss how militarism affects ecological issues, world hunger, racism, the role of the US in the global economic and political power struggle, the movement of women in other countries for peace and equality, and the role of spirituality in working for peace. We seek to develop a broad-based feminist peace politics, to work together effectively across race and class lines, and to share ideas for imaginative, effective actions we can take locally, regionally, nationally and internationally."

It said nothing about the speak-out, however. We couldn't anticipate the scene of that Wednesday, white women on one side of the room, women-of-color on another. First the women-of-color then the white women answering two questions: What do you absolutely adore about being (Mexican, Black, Native American, Jewish, White Anglo-Saxon . . .)? What is it that you never, ever as long as you live want to hear from women who look like the women on the other side of the room?

With over forty of us speaking out, it took all night. Organically, the need to speak out was acknowledged as tensions rippled through this group of uppity women, women used to speaking our hearts and minds and guts. I missed the events leading up to its proposal and acceptance. My grandmother's death took me away from the first half of the gathering, kept my mother away for its entirety. When I returned, the program had been derailed a night and a day, catalyzed by a showing of *Broken Rainbow*, a film about Big Mountain atrocities of mining and relocation of Dine people.

Few of us had ever spoken out like we did at the speak-out. I hadn't. Mary Arnold, in introducing the process, said it would be empowering. Mary Arnold, a member of an ongoing multicultural network in Iowa that works on internalized and externalized racism, was right.

We entered the process with an oath of confidentiality. So the only story I can tell without breaking that oath is my own. I was shaken by the suggestion that we divide ourselves along color lines—in this corner, women-of-color . . . I heard a woman to my right say she was glad we were doing with our bodies what was going on in our minds and hearts. I didn't like it. Said so.

Then we celebrated. What is it that I absolutely love about my self? Clothed in a flowing outfit handmade by a friend, I strutted. Said nothing. My 5'9" cherrywood being spoke for itself, arms outstretched to show off my lines. Then I danced as I sang a celebration of life that brought the house *up!* "And I love alla that," I said. And the fact that I survived Stanford Law School and can still love alla that. And that I have a mutually nurturing relationship with a Black man. And recognize my mother as the wise elder that she is. There is more, much much more.

After we each celebrated our selves, we got up to say what we never, ever, as long as we lived, wanted to hear from a white woman. With many colored sisters at my back, facing that crowd of white faces, some familiar, some loved, some simply white. With every cell threatening to go its own way. Fast. (What was *my* fear?) I said, "Don't tell me you understand what it means to be Black just because you've had a Black lover." After we were all done, the white women said what they heard. It was empowering to say to twenty-some white women what I'd never said to any white woman before, but wanted to. It was empowering to know we were heard, as several white women got up to reflect back to us our words and feelings.

It was empowering to hear what the white women there liked about themselves. And rare. Especially so since this was, after all, a "gathering." All too often, my encounters with white women at ecology/peace gatherings have been of a limited variety. Either they are so glad to see me there. Or they are so sorry there aren't more of me there. ("But," I never say, "there is only one of me on this entire planet.") Or they want to know the Black perspective on this or that. Or they want to tell me the trouble they've had convincing people-of-color that issues of ecology and peace are of the utmost importance.

To hear what the white women liked about themselves and what they never, ever, as long as they lived wanted to hear from a woman-of-color ever again—*that* was an education. One comment stuck in my heart and brought tears—that any woman would be denied the joy of learning another's dance because she had "white-skinned privileges . . ."

Something moved. This group of white women facing me

became more human, more women with hopes and dreams and fears and pains that I could see and feel. I became more of myself, able to revel in it. Close to telling folks who looked like folks who have a legacy of hurting folks who look like me to STOP IT. Something moved. Some little corner of consciousness was cleared out. Some possibility of trust, or at least of honesty, was created. Some ability to speak and listen to those we see as "other." All critical qualities and skills to develop as we work to create a world where environmental responsibility is as natural as breathing in a world controlled by folks who look and act like folks who have a legacy of hurting folks and plants and animals and entire ecosystems that share this planet with us.

Imagine. Attending an ecofeminist gathering where there is parity, no group being able to call it their thang to be done this way. No one or two bits of color there to be glad about, or wonder why they're there. As many different perspectives as there are people there, and the recognition of the need and eagerness to work at working together.

By design. Imagine how empowering it would be. Create it.

About the Contributors

ROBERT ARCHIBALD is president of the Missouri Historical Society.

RACHEL L. BAGBY is a writer, singer, and social activist living in Virginia.

WENDELL BERRY is the author of thirty-two works of fiction, poetry and essays. He farms a hillside in his native Henry County, Kentucky where he has lived for the last thirty years.

MURRAY BOOKCHIN is the director emeritus of the Institute for Social Ecology and has, for over thirty years, been a major spokesman for the ecology, appropriate technology, and anti-nuclear movements.

GEORGE BREWSTER, author of *Land Recycling and the Creation of Sustainable Communities*, is the executive director of the California Center for Land Recycling.

ROBERT COLES is professor of psychiatry and medical humanities at Harvard University and the author of over forty books.

WILLIAM CRONON is a professor of history, geography, and environmental studies at the University of Wisconsin in Madison. He was awarded a MacArthur Fellowship for his contributions to the study of nature and culture.

ANNIE DILLARD is a Pulitzer Prize–winning essayist and the author of numerous fiction and non-fiction works including *Pilgrim at Tinker Creek* and *Teaching a Stone to Talk*.

DIANNE DUMANOSKI, a long-time environmental journalist and co-author of *Our Stolen Future*, reported on emerging environmental issues for *The Boston Globe* for more than a decade.

EVAN EISENBERG writes books and articles for major magazines on topics ranging from music to the confluence of nature, culture and technology. He is a former gardener for the New York City Parks Department.

LOUIS FISCHER is a biographer, international journalist and long-time friend of Mahatma Gandhi.

ANN ARMBRECHT FORBES is an anthropologist who teaches in the Environmental Studies Department at Dartmouth College.

PETER FORBES is the TPL Fellow, a veteran of many conservation projects in New England, and a photographer.

ERIC FREYFOGLE is the Max L. Rowe Professor of Law at the University of Illinois, Urbana and the director of the Illinois Environmental Council.

JEAN GIONO was one of France's great writers whose prodigious literary output included stories, essays, poetry, plays, and over thirty novels. He lived in Provence most of his life, and died in 1970.

EDDY L. HARRIS is the author of three critically acclaimed books including the story of his solo canoe trip down the Mississippi River. He's a graduate of Stanford University and teaches at Washington University in Missouri.

GERALD HAUSMAN is a mythologist whose lifetime of researching and recording Native American stories has been compiled in seven books.

JAMES HILLMAN is a psychologist, scholar, lecturer and the author of ten books. He lives in northeastern Connecticut.

LINDA HOGAN, the author of *Dwellings*, *Power*, and other titles, has received the Oklahoma Book Award for fiction, the Colorado Book Award, and an American Book Award. A Chicksaw, she lives in Colorado.

STEPHEN KELLERT is the co-author, with E. O. Wilson, of *The Biophilia Hypothesis* and a professor at the Yale School of Forestry and Environmental Studies.

DANIEL KEMMIS is the director of the Center for the Rocky Mountain West. He has written two books on modern civic life.

VERLYN KLINKENBORG is on the editorial board of the *New York Times* and has written several highly acclaimed books, including *Making Hay* and *The Last Fine Time*. He lives in Massachusetts and Montana.

JAMES HOWARD KUNSTLER is the author of eight novels, an editor for *Rolling Stone,* and a frequent contributor to the *New York Times Sunday Magazine.* He lives in upstate New York.

ALDO LEOPOLD was a founder of the Wilderness Society and created the first wilderness area in America. His seminal work, *A Sand County Almanac,* was published in 1949, shortly after his death.

GENE LOGSDON farms in Upper Sandusky, Ohio and is the author of ten books about farming and culture.

BARRY LOPEZ is the author of nine books of fiction and non-fiction. He has received many literary awards including the National Book Award and lives in western Oregon.

JOANNA MACY is a Buddhist scholar, author, translator of Rilke, and an international workshop leader. She lives in Berkeley, California.

DONELLA H. MEADOWS is a nationally syndicated columnist on sustainability issues, a professor at Dartmouth College, a MacArthur Fellow, and an organic farmer.

BILL MCKIBBEN, former staff writer for the *New Yorker,* is also the author of three books on culture and the environment, including *The End of Nature.* He lives with his family in the Adirondacks.

N. SCOTT MOMADAY, the winner of the Pulitzer Prize for fiction, is an artist, playwright and musician who often returns to his Kiowa ancestry and landscape for inspiration. He lives in New Mexico.

HELEN AND SCOTT NEARING homesteaded in Vermont and Maine for more than fifty years and wrote dozens of books describing that experience.

GARY PAUL NABHAN has collaborated on twelve books, most of which deal with his beloved desert landscapes and culture. He is the director of research for the Sonora Desert Museum in Arizona.

RODERICK NASH is a professor of history and environmental studies at the University of California, Santa Barbara and the author of nine books that deal primarily with changing attitudes toward nature in the United States.

PENNY NEWMAN is currently the director of the Center for Community Action and Environmental Justice in Riverside, California.

MARY OLIVER lives on Cape Cod and is the author of more than a dozen books of poetry, including *American Primitive*, which won the Pulitzer Prize in 1983.

DAVID ORR is a professor of environmental studies at Oberlin College in Ohio, and the co-founder of the Meadowcreek Project, a nonprofit environmental education organization.

OLIVE PIERCE is a photographer and teacher residing on the coast of Maine and in Cambridge, Massachusetts.

MICHAEL POLLAN is the contributing editor of *Harper's Magazine* and lives in northwestern Connecticut.

ROBERT MICHAEL PYLE is the author of ten books and the winner of the John Burroughs medal for natural history writing. He lives in Gray's River, Washington.

ANTOINE DE SAINTE-EXUPÉRY was an author, philosopher, and pioneering pilot. Best known for his children's book *The Little Prince*, he disappeared in the summer of 1944 when his plane went down over the Mediterranean.

SCOTT RUSSELL SANDERS is the author of *Staying Put, Writing from the Center*, and other books. He teaches at Indiana University in Bloomington, where he lives.

E. F. SCHUMACHER is the author of *Small is Beautiful*, the best-selling reappraisal of Western economic attitudes. His pioneering work as an economist, journalist and progressive entrepreneur shaped society in Europe and America. He died in 1977.

SHEL SILVERSTEIN is the author of *The Giving Tree* and many other books of prose and poetry. He also writes songs, draws cartoons, sings, and plays the guitar.

GARY SNYDER has published sixteen books of poetry and prose and has won a Pulitzer Prize for poetry and a National Book Award for his essays. He lives next to the Tahoe National Forest in California.

WALLACE STEGNER was born in 1909 in Iowa but spent most of his adult life writing about, defining, protecting, and living in the American West. His fourteen books of fiction and non-fiction include *Angle of Repose*, which won the Pulitzer Prize.

JOHN STEINBECK is the author of many well-known novels, including *The Grapes of Wrath*, *Of Mice and Men*, and *East of Eden*.

BRIAN SWIMME is a popular physicist, author, and on the graduate faculty of the California Institute of Integral Studies in San Francisco.

HENRY DAVID THOREAU's late nineteenth-century writings on nature and society inspired the modern environmental movement as well as the civil rights and anti-apartheid movements.

HARRY S TRUMAN was president of the United States from 1945–53 after representing the state of Missouri in the Senate. He led the U.S. for the closing years of the Second World War and was an enthusiastic supporter of both the creation of the United Nations and the Marshall Plan.

JACK TURNER lives in the Tetons, and has traveled extensively in India, China, Tibet, and Pakistan. He is the author of a book of essays, *The Abstract Wild*.

RICHARD WHITE is a professor of history at the University of Washington where he teaches and writes about environmental history, western history, and Native American history.

HELEN WHYBROW is the editor in chief of The Countryman Press in Woodstock, Vermont, an imprint of W. W. Norton.

TERRY TEMPEST WILLIAMS is the naturalist-in-residence at the Utah Museum of Natural History in Salt Lake City and the author of *Refuge: An Unnatural History of Family and Place*.

DONALD WORSTER is the Hall Distinguished Professor of American History at the University of Kansas and author of *Rivers of Empire*, *Nature's Economy*, and other works of environmental scholarship.

Bibliography

Archibald, Robert. 1995. "The Places of Stories." *History News*, Vol. 52: 6, 7.

Bagby, Rachel L. 1990. "Daughter of Growing Things." In *Reweaving the World: The Emergence of Ecofeminism*, edited by Irene Diamond and Gloria Feman Orenstein. San Francisco: Sierra Club Books, 237, 241–243.

———. 1989. "A Power of Numbers." In *Healing the Wounds: The Promise of Ecofeminism*, edited by Judith Plant. Philadelphia: New Society Publishers, 93–95.

Berry, Wendell. 1981. *Recollected Essays 1965–1980*. San Francisco: North Point Press, 101–102, 104–105.

———. 1998. *The Selected Poems of Wendell Berry*. Washington, D.C: Counterpoint Press, 152.

———. 1992. *Sex, Economy, Freedom and Community*. New York: Pantheon, 171–172.

———. 1995. *Another Turn of the Crank*. Washington, D.C: Counterpoint Press, 49–51, 55–56, 74–75.

———. 1989. *The Hidden Wound*. San Francisco: North Point Press, 129.

Bookchin, Murray. 1982. *The Ecology of Freedom*. Palo Alto: Cheshire Books, 41–43.

Brewster, George. 1998. "Land Recycling and the Creation of Sustainable Communities," Policy Paper No. 1. San Francisco: California Center for Land Recycling.

Coles, Robert. 1967. *Children of Crisis: Migrants, Sharecroppers, Mountaineers*. Boston: Little, Brown, 3, 13–14, 23–24.

Cronon, William. 1983. *Changes in the Land: Indians, Colonists, and the Ecology of New England*. New York: Hill and Wang, 74–75, 80–81.

Dillard, Annie. 1982. *Teaching a Stone to Talk*. New York: Harper and Row, 150–152.

Dumanoski, Dianne. 1998. "Re-thinking Environmentalism." Malden, Mass.: Conservation Law Foundation, *Conservation Matters*, Fall 1998.

Eisenberg, Evan. 1998. *The Ecology of Eden*. New York: Alfred A. Knopf, 45–48, 57, 100–101, 158, 244, 253–255, 260, 358, 368, 378, 380–381, 428–430.

Fischer, Louis. 1950. *The Life of Mahatma Gandhi*. New York: Harper and Row, 230–233.

Forbes, Ann Armbrecht. 1997. "Thin Places." *Terra Nova*, Vol. 3: 112–114, 118.

Freyfogle, Eric. 1998. *Bounded People, Boundless Lands*. Washington, D.C.: Shearwater Press / Island Press, 3–6, 13–16, 173.

Giono, Jean. 1985. *The Man Who Planted Trees*. White River Junction, VT: Chelsea Green Publishing, 23–26 (*Vogue*, 1954).

Harris, Eddy L. 1997. "Solo Faces." *Outside Magazine*, Vol. 22, No. 12 (December), 108, 177–178.

Hausman, Gerald. 1992. *Turtle Island Alphabet: A Lexicon of Native American Symbols and Culture*. New York: St. Martin's Press, 81–83.

Hillman, James. 1983. *Inter Views*. Dallas: Spring Publications, 135–136.

Hogan, Linda. 1995. *Dwellings*. New York: W. W. Norton, 38–41.

Kellert, Stephen R. 1997. *Kinship to Mastery: Biophilia in Human Evolution and Development*. Washington, D.C.: Island Press

Kemmis, Daniel. 1995. *The Good City and the Good Life*. New York: Houghton Mifflin, 6–7, 12–14, 18, 123.

Klinkenborg, Verlyn. 1995. "Crossing Borders: Good News from the Badlands." *Audubon Magazine*, September 1995: 36–44.

Kunstler, James Howard. 1993. *The Geography of Nowhere: The Rise and Decline of America's Man-Made Landscape*. New York: Simon and Schuster, 10, 26–27, 238–241.

Leopold, Aldo. 1986. *A Sand County Almanac*. New York: Ballentine Books, 239–263 (New York: Oxford University Press, 1966).

Logsdon, Gene. 1993. *The Contrary Farmer*. Post Mills, Vermont: Chelsea Green Publishing, 44–45, 50–51.

Lopez, Barry. 1990. *Crow and Weasel*. San Francisco: North Point Press, 44–48, 61–63.

Macy, Joanna. 1991. *World as Lover, World as Self*. Berkeley, California: Parallax Press, 12–14.

McKibben, Bill. 1997. "Job and Wilderness." *Wild Earth*, Fall 1997: 7–8.

Meadows, Donella H. 1991. *The Global Citizen*. Washington, D.C.: Island Press, 281–283.

Momaday, N. Scott. 1997. *The Man Made of Words*. New York: St. Martin's Press, 45, 47–48.

Nabhan, Gary Paul. 1997. *Cultures of Habitat*. Washington, D.C.: Counterpoint Press, 37–38, 319.

Nash, Roderick. 1989. *The Rights of Nature*. Madison: University of Wisconsin Press, 212.

Nearing, Helen, and Scott Nearing. 1954. *Living the Good Life: How to Live Sanely and Simply in a Troubled World*. New York: Shocken Books, 84.

Newman, Penny. 1994. "Killing Legally with Toxic Waste." In *Close to Home: Women Reconnect Ecology, Health and Development Worldwide*, edited by Vandana Shiva. Philadelphia: New Society Publishers, 51–52.

Oliver, Mary. 1992. "Wild Geese." In *New and Selected Poems*. Boston: Beacon Press, 1992, 110.

Orr, David. 1998. "Speed." *Conservation Biology*, Vol. 12, No. 1, 6.

Pierce, Olive. 1996. *Up River: The Story of a Maine Fishing Community*. Hanover, N.H.: University Press of New England, 22.

Pollan, Michael. 1991. *Second Nature*. New York: Atlantic Monthly Press, 133–137.

Pyle, Robert Michael. 1993. *The Thunder Tree*. New York: The Lyons Press, 142–3, 145–147, 152.

Sanders, Scott Russell. 1993. "Staying Put." *Orion Magazine*, Vol. 4, 15–19.

Sainte-Exupéry, Antoine de. 1971. *The Little Prince*. New York: Harcourt Brace Jovanovich, 64–71.

Schumacher, E. F. 1979. *Good Work*. New York: Harper and Row, 1–4.

Silverstein, Shel. 1974. "Where the Sidewalk Ends." In *Where the Sidewalk Ends: The Poems and Drawings of Shel Silverstein*. New York: Harper and Row, 3.

Snyder, Gary. 1990. *The Practice of the Wild*. San Francisco: North Point Press, 14–15, 36–37, 152–154.

———. 1995. *A Place in Space*. Washington, D.C.: Counterpoint Press, 233–235.

Stegner, Wallace. 1998. *Marking the Sparrow's Fall: Wallace Stegner's American West*. New York: Henry Holt, 6, 112–117, 154–155, 156, 175–176.

Steinbeck, John. 1989. *The Grapes of Wrath*. New York: Viking Press, 87.

Swimme, Brian. 1996. *The Hidden Heart of the Cosmos*. Maryknoll, New York: Orbis Books, 12–18.

Thoreau, Henry David. 1958. *Walden*. New York: Harper Classics, 96 (Boston: Houghton Mifflin, 1854).

Truman, Harry S. 1957. "The Center of the World." Unedited audio transcript, aired on National Public Radio, Feb. 19, 1999.

Turner, Jack. 1996. *The Abstract Wild*. Tucson: University of Arizona Press, 91–93, 95, 100–101, 102.

White, Richard. 1995. "Are You an Environmentalist, or Do You Work for a Living?" In *Uncommon Ground*, edited by William Cronon. New York: W. W. Norton, 239–243.

Williams, Terry Tempest. 1995. "Testimony." *Wild Earth*, Winter 1995: 6–7.

Worster, Donald. 1997. "The Wilderness of History." *Wild Earth*, Fall 1997: 12–13.

Permissions Acknowledgments

Every effort has been made by the publisher to contact the sources of the selections in this book. Grateful acknowledgement is made for permission to reprint excerpts from:

Archibald, "The Places of Stories," © 1995 by Robert Archibald, reprinted from *History News*, Vol. 52.

Bagby, "Daughter of Growing Things," from *Reweaving the World*, © 1990 by Irene Diamond and Gloria Orenstein, reprinted with permission of Sierra Club Books; "A Power of Numbers" from *Healing the Wounds* © 1989 by Judith Plant, reprinted with permission of New Society Publishers.

Berry, "A Native Hill," from *Recollected Essays 1965–1980*, © 1981 by Wendell Berry, reprinted with permission of North Point Press / Farrar, Straus, and Giroux; passage from *Another Turn of the Crank*, © 1995 by Wendell Berry, reprinted with permission of Counterpoint Press / Perseus Books; "Conservation is Good Work," and "Conservation and Local Economy," from *Sex, Economy, Freedom, and Community*, © 1992 by Wendell Berry, reprinted with permission of Pantheon Books; "The Record," from *The Selected Poems of Wendell Berry*, © 1998 by Wendell Berry, reprinted with permission from Counterpoint Press / Perseus Books; passage from *The Hidden Wound*, © 1989 by Wendell Berry, reprinted with permission of North Point Press / Farrar, Straus, and Giroux.

Brewster, passage from "Land Recycling and Sustainable Communities" © 1998 by George Brewster, reprinted with permission of The California Center for Land Recycling.

Coles, passage from *Children of Crisis: Migrants, Sharecroppers, Mountaineers*, © 1967, 1968, 1969, 1971 by Robert Coles, reprinted with permission from Little, Brown and Company.

Cronon, passage from *Changes in the Land* © 1983 by William Cronon, reprinted with permission of Farrar, Straus and Giroux.

Dillard, passage from *Teaching a Stone to Talk*, © 1983 by Annie Dillard, reprinted with permission of HarperCollins Publishers.

Dumanoski, "Rethinking Environmentalism," © 1998 by Dianne Dumanoski, reprinted with permission of the author and The Conservation Law Foundation. The piece originally appeared in *Conservation Matters*.